Living in His Forgiveness

A Bible Study for Post-Abortive Women

D1361812

Sandy Day

with Carolyn McGuire

Living in His Forgiveness

A Bible Study for Post-Abortive Women
Sandy Day
with Carolyn McGuire

Unless otherwise noted, all Scripture is taken from
The New American Standard Bible
©1960, 1962, 1963, 1971, 1973, 1975, 1977, 1995
by The Lockman Foundation
Used by Permission

ISBN: 1-885904-42-8
Cover Design by Barbara Richards

PRINTED IN THE UNITED STATES OF AMERICA
by
FOCUS PUBLISHING
Bemidji, Minnesota 56601

Dedication

This book is dedicated to my parents

Leroy and Peggy Pittman

Thank you for your love and forgiveness.

Foreword

Dear Reader,

This book is a gift of God to you. Reading it reminded me of the time I was a nursing instructor (and unsaved) at a local college. A woman came to me and told me she was pregnant. Since she was married and had other children, and because I knew she had a very serious problem with high blood pressure, I said, "Oh, I'm sorry, but you know you need to have an abortion. Talk to your doctor." I do not know who else she talked to but she did have an abortion. I did not give it a second thought until after I was saved and the Lord convicted me of my part in influencing her. So I contacted her, met with her, gave her my testimony, and asked her forgiveness. She too expressed regret. How ashamed I was of my part in influencing her decision, but how thankful I was to the Lord that He had shown me my sin and renewed my mind to think rightly about God's precious gift of life.

Ladies, you can trust this material because it is biblically sound. God's Word is true, and as difficult as it is for any of us to admit our sin, therein lies our only hope. The hope of forgiveness, peace of mind, eternal life, and living a God-honoring life is presented clearly and in an engaging manner by Sandy Day and Carolyn McGuire. I highly recommend this book to you.

May God use it to bless you and for His glory,

Martha Peace
Author, *The Excellent Wife*

Acknowledgments

First of all, I would like to thank the Lord Jesus for the desire and opportunity to write such a book. He knows the many, many people who will benefit from it. I give Him all the glory and praise for His timing, for His provision of the right people in my life, and for moving us to California to complete it. He is truly an amazing God!

I am deeply grateful to Cindy Yager, Eddie O'Brien, Amy Niebuhr, Cynthia Fong, Brenda Ownbey, Debby Mylar, Kimberly Lorenzini, and Chris Nelson for allowing us to include their stories in this book. Each story is a testimony of God's love and compassion for the hurting, broken heart. Thank you for your willingness to be used of God to help others.

I appreciate all those who read the manuscript and offered helpful suggestions. Catherine Plough graciously helped in editing some of the stories. Several read the final draft to ensure accuracy and continuity: Dr. William Barrick; Suzanne Martin; Dr. Stuart Scott; and my precious husband, Craig Day who gave us appropriate verses at the final stages of our book and did much exegetical work for us. We thank you for all the time you spent!

I would like to thank all the special people at Focus Publishing. I want to thank them for having a heart to reach the post-abortive woman. You will make many, many women very grateful for all the time you have put into making this project happen. Special thanks to Jan, Barb and to Shelley for ALL the times you answered the phone when I called!

Last but not least I would like to thank my dear friend Carolyn McGuire. Your Bible knowledge, understanding of the scriptures, and your compassion for others made the Bible Study portions in this book what they are. I can't thank you enough for all you have done to make this book possible. You have blessed my life in abundance - you have helped others in ways that you will never know!

Table of Contents

Personally to you...

Dear Friend,

Through His Word, God has shown me that He has a purpose and meaning for my life even though I had made a mess of things by going my own way and doing my own thing. In Jeremiah 29:11-18 God explains His intention for those who are His children. "For I know the plans I have for you," declares the Lord, "plans for welfare and not for calamity to give you a future and a hope. Then you will call upon Me and come and pray to Me, and I will listen to you. And you will seek Me and find Me, when you search for Me with all your heart." It is the longing of my heart that you also would know the peace that only He can give regardless of what you have done in your past.

From my earliest years, my Mom and Dad thought I was a rather unusual child. I was high-strung and had a TON of energy! In today's world I would have had many labels added to my name. I remember one day when my Mom had taken me to 4-year-old pre-school. I didn't like what they were doing that day, so I left! I walked home. Even though the pre-school was less than a mile from our house, my Mom was, to say the least, not very happy to see me. In later years my energy was funneled into things that I thought would make me happy.

At age 13, I began a rebellious and promiscuous lifestyle, which included alcohol and drugs. By the grace of God I graduated from High School in 1977. Today, I realize that God protected me in many circumstances.

After graduation, I began dating a boy who came from a family that considered church a priority. Just to get his parents off my back, I went to church with them. That was where I heard the Gospel for the first time. As I learned about God's love and forgiveness, I knew I had a LOT to be forgiven! Two Sundays later, I responded to God drawing me to Himself. I called on the name of the Lord for my salvation and repented of my sin. God began to transform my life. I now had a desire to know God and His purposes for me. After confessing my sin, I knew I had to break off the relationship with my boyfriend because of our sinful involvement. Four weeks later I discovered I was pregnant.

I saw abortion as my only option. The moment the procedure was over, I knew I had made a terrible mistake - something that would have lifelong consequences. Today, I am still seeing those lifelong consequences. Like so many women in the world today, I learned to hide my pain. In a matter of months, I met a Christian man who became my husband. After we were married, we attended church and worked long hours to build a business together.

But all was not well. Two years into my marriage, I received a call at work from my husband. His message was: "I love you but I have to go." That day he ended his life. It was a tragedy that awakened me to the power of God's Word. God's Word became my "best friend." As I clung to God's promises, they saw me through the next leg of my journey, one perhaps even more difficult than the last.

After a leave of absence, I returned to my spot in the church choir. In my "usual" seat sat a woman I had never met. As we sat next to each other, we quickly became friends sharing our struggles and prayer requests. What I didn't know was that when I prayed for my friend's son, Craig - as I was often asked to do - I was praying for my second husband.

I was in the choir the Sunday night Craig gave his life to Christ. Amazingly, it was only a short time before he was ministering to me. Three years later we were planning a wedding and married on May 4, 1985.

Two and a half years into our marriage we conceived our first baby. One morning eight months into the pregnancy I realized something was wrong and called the doctor. I was told to come into his office. The doctor confirmed the worst; there was no heartbeat.

Three hours later we delivered our precious baby, James Caleb Day. The doctor explained that the cord was wrapped around his legs and had cut off his circulation and eventually ended our child's life. Today, my life and ministry revolve around the unwavering faith that God had a purpose for Caleb's life and death. At this point, we faced each day with sorrow and grief over the loss of our son. We had no idea what God had in store for us in the future with Caleb Ministries.

After losing Caleb, I was left with an intense desire for a child. God graciously brought me to the point where He was enough - with or without a baby. After hearing a message about Hannah one Sunday morning, I gave my deepest longing for a child to God. As only God could have timed it, that very night I discovered I was already pregnant with our second son, Corey.

It was a difficult pregnancy that required bed rest beginning in the fifth month. It was during those months on bed rest that God changed my perspective of who He is. I believed that God was punishing me for my past and for the terrible, promiscuous life I had led. Through doing a Bible study during that time, God revealed His character to me. He taught me the Truth of His unchanging love and healing forgiveness. By my delivery date, I had gained a new thankfulness for all I had experienced and a new appreciation for God's loving plan for me.

When Corey was about ten months old, God gave me a desire to begin a ministry to help other women who had endured losses. As Craig and I began to pray, we saw God put the ministry into place. People would call our home seeking help. Women's groups requested me to give the testimony of what God had done in our lives. God allowed us to comfort others with the comfort we had received from Him.

Over the years, I began to realize that a powerful testimony of God's saving grace and comfort was not enough for a powerful ministry to women. God wanted me to be a pure vessel so that I could be transparent with the women I sought to help. I began by agreeing to complete a Bible study that addressed issues I had tucked away for years and did not ever want to share with ANYONE! That study changed me forever as I received God's forgiveness and cleansing for the abortion that I had tried to hide.

Not long after completing that study, nine women called the ministry within a three-month period seeking help. Each woman had experienced a stillbirth and each one had an abortion in her past. Craig encouraged me to step out and share what God had done in my life to forgive my sin of abortion. As a result I have been so blessed by the opportunity to share God's answer for the silent pain women still live in due to their own abortion(s).

In 1999, my husband Craig accepted a call to Pastoral ministry. We moved to Southern California where he completed his Master's of Divinity Degree in May 2002 from The Master's Seminary. He presently pastors a church in Charlotte, NC.

Today, the ministry continues to grow. Letters expressing the pain in the hearts of women arrive in a continual stream. Now I am beginning to get letters from women who face the struggles of being a Pastor's wife. Sometimes I have to pinch myself to fully grasp that as one of my "roles." I really LOVE it all! Ministering to the lives that God has entrusted to us in our church is a privilege we take very seriously. The blessing of ministering to others is one of the rewards of serving Christ. However, my biggest blessing still comes from being a wife and mother. I thank the Lord for my godly husband. The Lord has used him in my life in so many ways; I would not have shared about my abortion without his encouragement. Our son Corey also has a heart to serve God and he brings us so much joy!

God also has a plan for you and has provided for your every need. He offers forgiveness to your soul and comfort for your heart. There is hope for the future. It is our prayer that as you read this book and answer these questions that God's Word will penetrate your heart and you will come to know His love and mercy. I rejoice with you in what God has in store for your life and the transformation He wants to shower upon you as you learn to live in His forgiveness.

Looking to Him for you,

Sandy

Chapter 1

"I acknowledged my sin to Thee,
And my iniquity I did not hide; I said, I will confess my transgressions to the Lord;
And Thou didst forgive the guilt of my sin."
Psalm 32:5

Forgiveness in Repentance

Stories of God's Grace

Day 1

A Quest for Love
Amy Niebuhr

I grew up the fourth of five children. Together we lived in a house - not a home. That's because our parents didn't love each other; in fact, they didn't even like one another. "Family" was not a word that would have described us. We were simply seven people living together. As early as five-years old, I can recall craving love and attention. I wanted what my friends had. I would even tell my parents lies so I would get their attention. As the years went by, that craving became an obsession. Once I became a teenager, I actively began my quest for someone to love me as I was, regardless of my faults. I began wearing sensual attire to attract men and lots of make-up to make myself look older. Before long I was dating much older men. Even though I was in high school, I hung around with a much older crowd where I was treated older as well. What I wanted was someone to comfort me when I was scared and to turn to for advice when I was faced with a difficult decision. I craved someone to meet my lustful desire for love and I thought if someone loved me that would meet those desires.

At sixteen I was sure I had found that love and security in a rela-tionship with a married man. Eventually when this man ended our relationship, I felt rejected and alone. It wasn't long before I was once again on my quest for love and happiness. Time and time again it was my own desperate desire for love that sabotaged my relationships. I could only conclude that my body was the only part of me worth loving and that I would have to settle for physical inti-macy alone. As a result, my relationships became completely phys-ical. There was no mutual respect; there was no dignity. This lifestyle would lead me into the darkest period of my life.

After a couple of years of this immoral life, I found myself preg-nant. One of my first thoughts was *"Who will love me now - with a baby? There is no way I can keep this baby if I ever want a happy life"*. There was only one solution. I terminated my pregnancy at 10 weeks. For about a week, I struggled emotionally with that decision, mourning my loss. But my desire for love was relentless, with a power even stronger than the guilt I had inflicted upon myself. The quest began again and finding love was, as it had always been, my deepest desire and my highest priority.

About two years later, I became involved in a relationship that I believed to be more than just physical. I felt certain I had found someone who really cared about me. I wanted this man to love me so badly that I would have done anything for him. And I did. After dating about six or seven months, I found myself pregnant again. When I told him the news, he was anything but excited. "How could you do this to me?" he responded accusingly. "If you care at all about me and our future you won't have this baby," he continued. All I heard in that statement was that there was, in fact, the possibility of a future together; there was hope that someone would love me. That was my dream. In my desperation I agreed to have an abortion. My boyfriend paid for it and even drove me to the clinic. That same evening, he went to a party and found himself a new girlfriend.

At home, I fell into a deep depression. I literally gave up. My feelings became numb and I didn't care about the ramifications of my actions. I grew certain that life was not worth living and thought many times about ending my life. But those emotions seemed to focus more and more on the loss of my children than on the loss of my most recent relationship. Guilt and shame overwhelmed me.

Though I tried not to think about it, evidence of what I had done seemed to meet me at every turn. Pictures of pre-born children drove me to tears. Then there was the fear. I was convinced in my heart that God would punish me and that I would never find true love.

A couple of years passed before I met the man I would eventually marry. My life to this point had been a series of self-destructive pursuits. The experience of undergoing two abortions left me feeling used, ugly, ashamed, unworthy of love, and deserving of ill treatment. In spite of my own feelings of worthlessness, God brought a precious gift into my life. I met a real "gentle man" whom God used to start me on a path toward a more stable life. I knew I did not deserve him and, in my fear of losing him, I kept my past a secret. It was my resolve that no one would ever know.

The stress of keeping this secret became unbearable, however. During the years that followed, when I heard the topic of abortion discussed, or even the word mentioned, I reacted strongly cringing both physically and emotionally. In time I developed what I thought was an effective strategy for dealing with the pain; I just pretended it never happened. It worked so well that I almost believed it myself. Almost!

With my secret past locked away, Chris and I were married in 1993. Two years later we moved to Charleston, South Carolina where I met a very dear friend, Anita Couch. I was three months pregnant with our second child when Anita invited me to attend a Caleb Ministries Women's Retreat that would take place in November. In God's providence, I agreed to go. Having no idea what to expect, I sat down to hear a testimony given by a woman named Chris Nelson. (Her story is in this book.) Just as Chris began to speak, I knew in my heart that this was why I was there. I listened carefully as Chris told the story of her own abortion. All I could do was sob in my amazement as I realized that God knew everything about me. My soul was laid bare before Him as I heard God's declaration in the Scriptures. **"For My eyes are on all their ways; they are not hidden from my face, nor is their inequity hidden from My eyes" (Jeremiah 16:17- NKJV).** I wanted so badly to "come clean" to somebody; and yet, I was battling the enemy's lie: Abortion is the unforgivable sin. An opportunity came to receive prayer. Half on and half off the seat, I wanted desperately to pray with someone - anyone!

My internal battle raged on. Eventually all I could hear was the voice of fear. *"Are you crazy? These people will judge you! You don't want all these people you just met to know this about you. It has been a secret this long - just keep it that way."* I struggled to convince myself not to rock the boat while not wanting to carry that load of guilt any longer. In the midst of my turmoil, a friend turned and asked me if I would like to go somewhere private to pray. I managed to nod my head. But as we sat in the corner and she prayed with me, the struggle continued. I worried that my husband would be angry if I told someone else before he knew. So I determined to explain my tears by "admitting" my fear of losing the baby I was carrying. That is what I did; I lied to her face. At that moment, fear of the consequences of telling the truth was stronger than my desire to be free from guilt. Once back in my room, I reasoned that I would open up to my friend, Anita. But again, I gave into fear, pretending to be asleep when she returned to the room.

The next morning, November 16, 1997, my life was changed forever. That was the day God unlocked the room in which my secret had been kept for so many years. He exposed my sinful heart and gave me the courage to acknowledge and take responsibility for the sins I had committed throughout my life. I begged for His forgiveness and accepted Jesus' payment for my sins. When I acknowledged Christ as my Lord and Savior, I was a changed woman. He took the guilt and the shame from me in an instant. I knew I could no longer go my own way and I committed myself to God's way for my life. For the first time, I felt that I could breathe deeply. I felt very safe, secure, and warm inside. When someone becomes a Christian, he or she becomes a brand new person inside with a new desire to know and please God. A new life begins on a spiritual plane at that moment (1 Corinthians 5:17).

> **"Then, I acknowledged my sin to you and did not cover up my iniquity. I said, 'I will confess my transgressions to the Lord' - and you forgave the guilt of my sin."**
> **Psalm 32:5 (NIV)**

I was now alive spiritually with a new heart, but I returned home to a non-Christian husband. Though I was aware that the Lord would give me courage, I dreaded telling my husband the truth about my past. As I began to explain the decision I had made that very morning and the newfound freedom I had from exposing my hidden pain, he did not understand. Instead, he became suspicious about what else I had failed to share with him over the years. Very quickly we decided not to discuss it any further. It seemed my announcement had come at an inopportune time, just two days before our first family vacation. Throughout that vacation we avoided the subject and just went on as usual, though both our hearts were aching inside.

It was weeks after we returned from our vacation before we actually discussed my decision to follow Christ. God had used our vacation time to work in my husband's heart. Thankfully, he was willing to forgive my past. "If God can forgive you," he said, "then who am I to place judgment?" In the weeks that followed, my husband started asking questions about what it meant to have a relationship with Jesus Christ. Each day brought more questions. He asked questions about the inconsistencies he saw in people who claimed to be Christians, as well as questions about things he did not understand in the Bible. He recognized that he didn't have the love for God that he saw in people at church and yet he had prayed the prayer to become a Christian. Finally, he asked to meet with my friend, Anita, and the Lord used her to address his questions from God's Word. Within a few days, he made his decision to accept God's gift of salvation.

Our decisions to follow Christ have caused us to see every area of our lives in a new light - the light of God's Word! Today, "our family" has a whole new meaning. As we walk this incredible journey together, we have grown closer to Christ, closer to one another and closer to His people in His Church. My husband and I began attending Bible studies where we developed friendships with others who love the Lord. We are filled with the assurance that we have been forever changed, and with peace knowing we will never walk alone. I am so thankful to my Lord for giving us the courage to be obedient.

That day in November, my birthday into God's family, ended my lifelong quest for love; for I found all that I needed - in abundance - in Jesus Christ. I look back and realize that His love was mine for the asking all those years when I was searching. Throughout my quest, God was the source of the very love that I was so desperately seeking. It was His lovingkindness that brought me to repentance - not to condemn me, but to save me (Romans 8:1). It was His pursuit of me that allowed me to find relief from my guilt and shame. I am now free from them through Jesus Christ who paid the price of my guilt.

In my thankfulness, I pray for young girls who are so focused on love as I was. I pray they would come to recognize their real need of a Savior to forgive their lustful craving for love and change their heart's desire to be pleasing to God. I also pray for women who carry the secret of an abortion in their past. I pray they would come to understand that God forgives sin - all sin! If this is your situation, seek out someone with whom you can talk about the guilt and grief that plagues you - a pastor, a pastor's wife, a godly counselor. God can use the very experience you are afraid to disclose to anyone to draw you into a loving relationship with Himself. God has replaced my desperate craving for love with a deep quest to love and serve Him.

Amy's UPDATE:
Amy and her husband Christopher reside in Mount Pleasant, SC with their two children. They are actively involved with a ministry that teaches parenting skills. After completing a post-abortion study Amy has the desire to share her story with others who are hurting, espe-

cially teens. Amy leads our post–abortion ministry, Abbey's Place, in the Charleston, SC Caleb Chapter.

Personally to you...

1. How were you encouraged after reading Amy's story?

2. At what point(s) did you identify with her story?

3. Below are a few Scripture passages Amy used. Which one(s) could you apply to your circumstances? How do they help you?

   • Jeremiah 16:17

   • I Corinthians 5:17

   • Psalm 32:5

Day 2

Too Late to Go Back
Eddie O'Brien

Not long ago, I stood talking with a few of my friends after church, most of them women. It was "Sanctity of Human Life" Sunday (See Day 3). Following the worship service, we discussed the nature of so many ungodly relationships that result in painful consequences for men and women; too often they also victimize an unborn child.

Most of the comments pointed the finger at men, many of whom support abortion as a solution for an unplanned pregnancy. "Women like romance, but men are just interested in one thing," was one woman's remark. Still another insisted, "Women are pushed into sexual relationships by men; they feel forced to give in to keep the man's acceptance." Then came the most devastating of the comments made: "I can't believe a man can get a girl pregnant and then blow it off, saying it's as easy as having an abortion - problem solved." I couldn't deny it. In fact, I had heard some of my own friends say those very words: "No problem, just tell her to have an abortion."

"Not all men are like that," I heard myself say. But it was at that moment that I realized I could have easily been the very man to offer such advice - or take it - had it not been for my own childhood experiences. I had seen, firsthand, the pain men could inflict on women. But as a man I had also learned that a woman's choice to thoughtlessly destroy a relationship and the life of an unborn child can have devastating effects for both partners.

My mother and father divorced when I was eight years old. A year later, my mother remarried. My stepfather was an alcoholic with a violent temper. Even when I couldn't see them, I heard the fights and the screams at my mother and sister. I knew that he would hurt them, and he did - broken fingers and ribs, black eyes, and blood. Holes in the walls and broken furniture marked the battlefield that was our home. I never knew a man could have such strength. Once

I dressed in my army costume, as a soldier prepared for war, and walked right up to my stepfather, commanding him to stop. His answer was to shove me against the wall. I could only walk away feeling angry and powerless.

A year later, on Valentine's Day, I had another chance to stand up to my stepfather. Apparently, my mother had called the police to our house by reporting my stepfather's threats. When she pointed at me, demanding, "Ask him, he'll tell you what happened," I was so afraid I couldn't say a word. The police left and I thought it was all over until my mother returned to the room with a pistol pointed at her chest. She threatened to shoot herself if my stepfather didn't leave immediately. He did leave, but she continued to point the gun at herself. I pleaded with her to put the gun down, even asking her to consider what God would say about what she was doing. This stunned her so that she abruptly turned to leave the room. It was then that she bumped into the door, setting off the gun. I ran to catch her, but I could not save her.

After the funeral I packed a suitcase and never went back to that house. Since I was only 15 years old, I moved in with my sister for awhile, and later with my father. I refused any offer of comfort; drugs and alcohol became my closest companions. Although I cared about very little back then, I decided in my heart that I would never abuse a woman. I made a commitment to treat women with respect. And I did, only to discover that gentlemen weren't in demand in my world. My efforts to please women only led to being rejected again and again.

By my senior year of high school, I found my way to be popular; I became a drug dealer. I was the life of the parties. Everyone wanted to be my friend when I had what they wanted. Even the girls began to flirt with me and I no longer got dumped all the time. It was a short-lived happiness, though. After I graduated, which was in itself a miracle, the friends that depended on me for their habits slowly began to disappear. I never expected anyone to really grow up and get jobs or go to college. I found myself in a desperate search for happiness. Cars, money, drinking, parties, all was a vain attempt to escape reality and create a world where I wouldn't get hurt. It was only a matter of time.

We had only been together for one night, and she got pregnant. All of my friends said, "No problem, just pay for her to have an abortion." They told me I was too young to be a father. A few hundred dollars would fix the mistake, if I shopped the abortion clinics for the best deal. I can't say I did not think about it, but the thought of a child, my own child, made me feel happy. It occurred to me that maybe this was what made life worthwhile. I told my girlfriend I'd be honored to be father to the child.

Unfortunately, her friends had given her other advice. One day, she handed me an informational brochure on abortion procedures and asked me to read it. Everything inside me resisted. "You can't do this - not to a baby or to yourself," I insisted. She reassured me that she was just curious.

However, shortly thereafter she informed me that it was "over." When I responded, "What is over?" her cold reply was, "I'm not pregnant anymore." I felt as though life went out of me. I could not believe she had killed our baby, my baby. There was nothing I could do; it was too late. In the end she left me for one of her friends who recommended the abortion.

It's hard to describe the emptiness that followed. I thought I had nothing else to lose, but I was wrong. Every day that passed, I gave another piece of my soul to the world. My thoughts constantly replayed that horrible scene of my mother's death, and then turned to images of an abortionist stealing life from a helpless baby. I couldn't get drunk enough - or high enough - to escape the relentless battle that raged in my mind.

Where was God? I had believed in Him. I always knew God was real and He was out there somewhere watching me. I had been baptized as a child and grew up in church. However, I had since developed my own religion, one that would justify my lifestyle. I decided that since I talked to God, I didn't need to read the Bible. I didn't need to go to church because it was full of hypocrites and I would never be like that. I figured God understood my drinking and all, since it was the only thing that helped me forget my pain.

Oh, how deceived I was. I was so good at telling lies to myself and others that I began to believe them over time. I convinced myself that my stepfather was not to blame for what happened to mom; that Mom was okay, watching over me in Heaven with God; and, that there remained in me no bitterness because my experiences had made me a stronger person. This is happiness, I reasoned.

True, I acknowledged that God was there, but I failed to recognize that my sin kept me from a relationship with a Holy God. I had heard about God as a child, but when tragedy struck, I looked to the world for comfort. I did not have a relationship with Jesus Christ.

At 27, I married Jennifer. With our union came her five-year-old son Matthew, from a previous marriage. Together we went to church, but just so Matthew would have a church upbringing. We only went for his sake. One Sunday, following an extended absence from the pulpit, our pastor brought the congregation some heart-wrenching news. His newborn daughter "Abbie" had been born with Downs Syndrome and a life-threatening hole in her heart. We watched, in amazement, as this man wept before us and gave the Lord his burdens. Tears poured down my face. Joy and sadness intertwined.

That day, God deeply impressed my heart with the Pastor's response to his circumstances. I hardly remember what the pastor said, but I will never forget the tears of gratitude he shed as he lifted his hands to praise the One who was his Refuge. He praised God even as his newborn baby lay dying; expressing his assurance that God was in control. I longed to know God like that. I didn't think I could live another day without what he had. I wanted Jesus so badly I could just die, and I did. That day, a sinful hard-hearted man of the world visited church and never left; but a new, forgiven man stood and walked out as a child of the King. Jesus became my Savior that day.

Having left the church when my Mom died, I had substituted my idea of God for the true God. Even though we were just going to church because Matt needed it, God knew we were the ones who needed it. God opened my spiritual eyes to know who God is, holy and just, to see myself as a sinner, and to accept Christ's death on the cross to provide forgiveness for my sin. **"I have been crucified with Christ; and it is no longer I who live, but Christ lives in me; and the life which I now live in the flesh I live by faith in the Son of God, who loved me, and delivered Himself up for me" (Galatians 2:20).**

The old self-rationalizing man has passed away, and, praise God, I am born anew to peace with God and a life of abundant blessing. Nothing in my past changed. My mother still died a horrible death, and I saw every second of it. Years were wasted in pain and loneliness hoping some bottle would numb the memories. The life of an unborn child was taken. But none of these experiences left me a stronger man. I was not wiser for my sinful decisions. It took Jesus to change me. That is the greatest part of my history: I didn't do anything; I couldn't. Jesus reached down into the filth of my shameful life and rescued me. He cleansed me with His own blood and brought stability to my life so that I could stand the storms of life.

Nothing within me could ever forgive those who had hurt me. I could not escape the guilt I felt for letting that baby die. I didn't even know how I could face life another day. Without Christ, I was utterly doomed under the penalty of my sin. My Lord and my Savior forgave me first, then Jesus placed inside of me His Grace and His Mercy so that I, too, could forgive. I had never known joy and happiness apart from Jesus, but I found freedom and security in my relationship with Him. Oh, how refreshing is the peace of abiding in Him!

> **"I am the Vine, you are the branches; he who abides in Me, and I in him, he bears much fruit; apart from Me you can do nothing."** **John 15:5**

Eddie's Update:
Eddie graduated with an Associates of Divinity degree from Southeastern Baptist Theological Seminary in May 2000. He is currently working on his Bachelor of Arts Degree in Biblical Studies and plans to go on to the Master of Divinity degree. Eddie and his wife, Jennifer, have done short-term mission work in India. They hope to serve there again in the future. They are so grateful for the way God has blessed their lives.

Personally to you...
1. How were you encouraged after reading Eddie's story?

2. At what point(s) did you identify with his story?

3. Below are a couple Scriptures from Eddie's story. Which one(s) could you apply to your circumstance(s)? How do they bring you comfort?

   • Galatians 2:20

   • John 15:5

Day 3

"Sanctity of Life" Sunday and Mother's Day
How do we get through them?

As I walked into the church, I thought "Oh no, it's THAT day again." They handed me a rose and I just wanted to run! The memories hurt so badly and I feel as though there is no one who understands my pain. People cannot imagine how painful this day is for women like me; women who have had an abortion or who have lost a baby? I can't imagine sitting through another service where they are going to talk about babies that have been murdered; they are going to call me "a murderer" AGAIN. If they knew how hurtful that is, I think they should have more compassion. I'm not sure they care. They only call us "murderers" and report the number of babies aborted since the passing of Roe vs. Wade. I don't want to hear that ever again. I think I will leave now. I turn to my husband and say, "Honey, can we leave?" But his reply is, "Sandy, it's going to be 'OK.' You will be fine." I never have walked out of church on either Mother's Day or Sanctity of Life Sunday, but I can tell you, that it was only as I tried to focus on Scripture that I was able to stay there. Many times I would sit in the pew with tears rolling down my cheeks.

Have you ever had thoughts like these? Even now, on these Sundays, my first urge is to run out of the church and come back the following Sunday. For me Mother's Day has been the hardest. When I purpose to "take my thoughts captive" (2 Corinthians 10:5) and look to God for His comfort and strength, He has surely given it to me. On those Sundays when no comforting words were offered to women who have lost babies through miscarriage, stillbirth, early-infant death or abortion, I have had to focus on God's forgiveness and lovingkindness that is new every morning. When you focus on what has happened to you, the pain is piercing, but when you fix your eyes on Jesus who was pierced for you and because of you, you can know the peace that is beyond understanding. In the next few paragraphs, I want to tell you some of the things that have helped me through the years.

First of all, if a certain day has been difficult for you in the past, plan ahead. If you are married ask your husband to pray with you and for you. Any close Christian friend might be willing to help you bear this burden.

Second, prepare key verses to meditate on during the service. These are a few that are special to me:

> **"There is therefore now no condemnation for those who are in Christ Jesus."**   **Romans 8:1**

> **"In my distress I called upon the Lord, and cried to my God for help; He heard my voice out of His temple, and my cry for help before Him came into His ears."**
> **Psalm 18:6**

> **"Behold, God is my helper; The Lord is the sustainer of my soul."**   **Psalm 54:4**

Third, you might prepare ahead by reading Jerry Bridge's book entitled *Trusting God*. It has helped me to understand much about God's sovereign plan for my life. Knowing that God knew the sin I would commit and yet He loved me and died in my place is over-whelming at times. In faith I am counting on His promise to work even this together for my good and His glory. As I think about His unconditional love that is like a special gift-wrapped package beautifully decorated with forgiveness, hope, and comfort for me, I am filled with tremendous gratitude and joy.

Finally, you could make an appointment with your pastor to help him recognize how painful these days are for many women who are sitting in His congregation. This awareness may help him to sensitively minister God's words of comfort and encouragement to those who long to hear them. This is a way for you to share the comfort you have received from the message of God's love and the joy of His forgiveness.

Remember, my friend, you are not alone on these days. There are many women who are hurting just as you are in every church. More importantly, God is there with you and for you. He knows your every heartache as it fits into His plan for you and He is even now working it together for your good. As we look to Jesus, we are reminded that He too suffered tremendous pain in being obedient to God's plan for our benefit. **"He was despised and forsaken of men, a man of sorrows, and acquainted with grief" (Isaiah 53:3).** His grief allows Him to understand our grief and to know how sorely we are tempted to despair. Today draw near to the One Who is our comfort, our strength, and Who wants to carry your burden for you.

Personally to you...

1. How do Mother's Day and/or Sanctity of Life Sunday affect you?

2. If you know the Lord Jesus as your personal Savior and have received His forgiveness, focusing on the following scriptures verses will inform and help balance your painful emotions. Write what each verse means to you:

   "Therefore there is now no condemnation" (Romans 8:1).

   "I will give you a new heart and put a new spirit within you" (Ezekiel 36:26).

"When I kept silent, my bones wasted away...and you forgave the guilt of my sin" (Psalm 32:3a-5b NIV).

"He brought them out of darkness and the deepest gloom" (Psalm 107:14-15 NIV).

"You shall know the truth and the truth shall set you free" (John 8:32,36 NIV).

"Forget the former things; do not dwell on the past..." (Isaiah 43:18-19 NIV).

Day 4

Lost But Found
Cindy Yager

I would be reluctant to tell you about my life were it not that God has completely changed it. I am going to share some very intimate and personal details that may shock you; some things you may have experienced yourself. My purpose in writing is three fold. First, I want to obey God and share the comfort I have received from Him. Second, I want you to know the joy of surrender that I have found. Third, I hope you will rejoice with me in what God has done with someone as wretched as I am. When we have gone through trials, we are able to encourage others who have had similar experiences. I want my story to point you to the Source of true hope.

I was raised in a large Catholic family. When I was young, my mother would take all six of her kids to church every Sunday. As a youngster, I knew about God and I had some desire to please Him; I even had the childhood notion of becoming a nun. Standards of right and wrong were instilled in me. I wanted to be good and tried to do good things. Looking back at my growing up years, it seems as though we had a relatively good family life.

Even though we were a typical American family that did fun things together, we also had our struggles. My mother was diagnosed with MS as a young woman, even before I was born. I was the fifth of six children and my earliest memories of my mother are of her in a wheelchair most of the time. We all eventually responded to this in our own way. My older brothers and sisters started getting into trouble, having problems in school, and getting into bad relationships, but I was determined to "be good." I was a good student, a cheerleader, and was crowned Homecoming queen in high school, but inside I felt empty and lonely. I sensed something was missing, but I didn't know how to fill up the void. While I longed to feel loved and to be happy, I was confused by my feelings and the nagging questions that filled my mind. I certainly never felt loved at church; I only felt guilty and not quite good enough. By the time I was in junior high, I had stopped going to church and turned my back on God as I perceived Him. I thought I could find love and happiness elsewhere.

At that time, I had very little knowledge of God as revealed in the Bible. You see I didn't know God as the One who spoke the world into existence. (Genesis 1:3) I didn't know that God said **"Before I formed you in the womb I knew you" (Jeremiah 1:5a)**. I didn't know that the first complex, detailed, wonderful human being came into existence when **"the Lord God formed man of the dust of the ground, and breathed into his nostrils the breath of life; and man became a living being" (Genesis 2:7 - NKJV).** I also didn't know that because that first man chose to disobey God, that I had inherited his sin nature and deserved to be separated from God forever. I had heard about Adam and Eve, but I didn't really understand how they had any effect on me. After all, the Bible was written so long ago, it could have nothing to do with me! I thought God was very obscure and did not know and could not possibly imagine that He wanted to have a personal relationship with me.

When I was about 13 years old, I found out how wonderful I could feel when I was high on alcohol and drugs. This became my escape so that I could forget about the pain inside and just "have fun." In my desperation, I sought and found it wherever I could. At 15 I got into a relationship with an older guy; that's when I lost my virginity. Having very little information about sex or birth control, my immorality led to pregnancy at 16. I chose to have my first abortion. I knew my parents would be devastated, so I never told them. Even though I knew it was wrong, I could not bear to hurt or disappoint my parents. At that time, that seemed like the most important thing.

Throughout high school, I continued to use drugs and alcohol but managed to maintain a "good" image on the outside. Right before graduation, I was pregnant again and this time decided to get married at 18 years old. My parents had already been disappointed by one of my siblings who had made bad choices. In my predicament I could see no other way out. You see, I didn't know that God had plans for me. **"Plans for welfare and not calamity to give (me) a future and a hope."** I didn't know that God had already promised, **"Then you will call upon Me and come and pray to Me, and I will listen to you. And you will seek Me and find Me, when you search for Me with all your heart" (Jeremiah 29:11-13).** I was searching for something, but in all the wrong places, and my search was only half hearted. I was so lost.

We were married and our little boy was born. He was precious. I poured my life into him for the first year or two hoping that this little baby would fulfill my selfish longings. Our son had to have two different surgeries and we had no medical insurance. Our financial struggles spiraled out of control because my husband's work was sporadic. By the time I became pregnant again, I had decided that I needed to go to work to ease our financial stress. I sent our son off to day care and got a job. Soon after our daughter was born, I decided I needed to get more schooling. While I was working full time, I started to attend school at night. I was again searching for something more out of life - more money, more security, more, more, more.

As I searched for more, my marriage was falling apart. I had become resentful and bitter towards my husband for not making enough money to support us. Rather than being supportive and encouraging him, I started giving him ultimatums and threatening to leave him if he didn't get a full time job. Around that time I became pregnant again. I decided that we just could not handle another baby and I chose to have my second abortion. By now my heart was becoming very hardened; God was the farthest thing from my mind. I just wanted to get on with my life. I was an example of Isaiah 53:6 that says, **"All of us like sheep have gone astray; each of us has turned to his own way; but the Lord has caused the iniquity of us all to fall on Him."** As I was independently "doing my own thing" and making my own decisions, God had no place in my life and I had no thought of his plans for me.

Going my own way included becoming involved with a married man and asking my husband for a divorce after seven years of marriage. I was so focused on my own happiness and fulfillment that I did not realize how a divorce would have lifelong consequences for my husband, my children, and me. I did not understand the meaning of the "marriage covenant" that God had designed, nor did I know that God said He hated divorce in Malachi 2:16. I was about to find out why.

As I continued in the adulterous relationship I believed all the promises of an affluent lifestyle; a big expensive home, a future with everything I thought I wanted. During that relationship, I became pregnant with his child and aborted that baby merely to avoid the embarrassment to both of us. So when that relationship ended, I was devastated. Now, I had no husband, no companion, and nothing

was working out the way I wanted, or the way I had tried to manip-
ulate it. I was clueless about God's plans for me that are spoken of
in Jeremiah 29:11, **"I know the plans that I have for you, declares
the Lord."** God who had "wove me in my mother's womb, had seen
my unformed substance, and written the days that were ordained for
me in His book when as yet there was not one of them" (Psalm
139:13-16). Before I was born, God who knows everything knew all
about me; I just did not know about Him yet.

Not knowing God and without a human companion, I was 26
years old and all alone. I did have two children, who at this point
were very angry with me. I could barely keep my head above water
now that all of my sinful, self-centered choices were beginning to
catch up with me. I had a business that was failing, a trail of failed
relationships, and I was failing as a mom. I became overwhelmed
with the physical, spiritual, and emotional pressures in my life.
Exhausted, afraid, and emotionally bankrupt, I moved back into my
parent's home. They graciously supported me and my children
through a period of about two years, while I slowly began to "get
my life back together."

I was able to get out from under my business and went to work
for a big company. Things were looking up, I thought.
Unfortunately I was still doing things my way, completely inde-
pendent of God. I soon fell back into my old behaviors of drinking
and using drugs to ease my pain and fill my loneliness. I didn't know
that **"When I kept silent about my sin, my body wasted away through
my groaning all day long. For day and night Thy hand was heavy
upon me; my vitality was drained away as with the fever heat of
summer" (Psalm 32:3-4).** I wanted to be a good person, but it
seemed that the harder I tried, the worse I failed. I couldn't do anything right.

Romans 10:9 says **"If you confess with your mouth Jesus as Lord,
and believe in your heart that God raised Him from the dead, you
shall be saved; for with the heart man believes, resulting in righteousness, and with the mouth he confesses, resulting in salvation."**
Despite all of my sin, He stood ready to forgive me, but I was not
yet ready to admit my sin to Him.

While I was working at my new job, I was attracted to a man
who seemed different from other guys I had known. We hit it off
right away and we talked about a lot of different things, including
God. When he asked me if I would like to go to church with him,
I said "Sure." He asked me a lot of questions about what I believed

and what I thought about God. At that point in my life, I wasn't really sure what I believed. I knew that I believed that there was a God, but I hadn't given Him much thought for a long time. Inside I felt afraid of God. I was filled with guilt and shame from my life, but I didn't even recognize it as that because I had rationalized everything for so long. We continued dating and then we became engaged to be married.

The pastor of the church where Darren and I were regularly attending required a six-month pre-marital class before he would marry us. Although we both knew we had many strikes against us going into marriage, we were determined to make it work. Darren was eight years younger than I was. I was divorced with two children ages nine and eleven. During one of our pre-marital sessions, the pastor asked me if I knew for sure that when I died, I would go to heaven. I said, "I hope I would, but no one can really know for sure." When he asked me if I wanted to know for sure, of course I said, "Yes." He then told me that the Bible said I could know for sure that I would go to heaven. In 1 John 5:13 the Bible promises that if I would confess my sins and accept Jesus' death as the payment for my sins, I would be forgiven and I would have a place in heaven with Christ when I died. It seemed easy enough to me; I did want to go to heaven, so I prayed with him and that was the green light for us to get married. I thought, "Now I am a real Christian" God had gotten my attention again, and I was determined to do well.

For about the first year of our marriage, things seemed to go pretty well. We had built a new home and I was trying to build a new life. On the outside everything seemed to be fine, but inside our home and our lives, there were deep-rooted problems. My children were very angry about my divorcing their dad and resented my marrying Darren. When I look back, I now see how blind I was to think that it would all "work out" and we would be one big happy family. It seemed like the harder I tried to be a good mom, and a good wife, the worse things got. Romans 7:19 describes my dilemma. **"For the good that I wish, I do not do; but I practice the very evil that I do not wish."** I was still in bondage to my sin and didn't know it.

Soon my "perfect" marriage was falling apart. Darren wanted out, and my kids didn't want to do anything but make our lives miserable. They were succeeding at that. The daily tension in our home was so thick you could cut it with a knife. The thought of another divorce and the level of stress in our home was driving me farther and farther from the happiness I sought. I would cry almost every day. My emotions were out of control and sometimes I even thought that if I could just die the pain would go away.

During this time of despair, I remember driving to work one day and crying so hard that I had to pull over because I couldn't see the road anymore. I began crying out to God and telling Him that I couldn't do it anymore. As I admitted that I couldn't run my life anymore, I finally asked Him to do as He pleased with it. God and I had this mental conversation. "God, what do you want?" I asked Him, wanting to know what I had to do. He said, "Surrender everything." I said, "Everything?" He said, "Yes, everything." I said, "What if I lose my husband, what if I lose my kids?" (at this point I had already lost them anyway) He said, "Not only do I want you to surrender them, but I want you, all of you!" I took a deep breath and said, "OK, I am ready. I can't do it anymore and I'm ready to turn everything over to you, God." Everything I had tried to do was a mess; my whole life was a mess. I could see no other way out. **"And He inclined to me and heard my cry. He brought me up out of the pit of destruction, out of the miry clay; and set my feet upon a rock making my footsteps firm. And He put a new song in my mouth, a song of praise to our God" (Psalm 40:1-3).**

After that prayer, I wasn't sure what I was going to do next. A feeling of great peace had come over me for the first time in my life. It was as if a huge burden had been lifted off me and I felt free. Romans 6:22-23 says, **"But now having been freed from sin and enslaved to God, you derive your benefit, resulting in sanctification and the outcome eternal life. For the wages of sin is death, but the free gift of God is eternal life in Christ Jesus our Lord."** I had finally realized that there was nothing that I could do to "work" my way to God or into heaven. I needed to turn from going my way to obeying God and accepting His payment for my sin by faith. It was not a really dramatic experience. I went to work that day and on the outside everything was still the same. My problems didn't go away, but my heart was different. Little by little I began to change. I knew I needed to depend on God for everything. God had me right where He wanted me, on my knees crying out to Him in humility. From that point on, I knew that I was His child and that nothing could separate me from Him again no matter how bad my life became. God had promised, **"Then I will sprinkle clean water on you, and you will be clean; I will cleanse you from all your filthiness and from all your idols. Moreover, I will give you a new heart and put a new spirit within you; and I will remove the heart of stone from your flesh and give you a heart of flesh" (Ezekiel 36:25-26).** For the first time I understood what it meant to make Jesus Christ the Lord and Savior of my life. He was now my Master.

I started reading my Bible to receive my Master's instructions. Each morning I would open it to learn from Him. Every time there would be something that I needed for that day. God's encouraging and comforting words began to make sense for the first time. I also started to pray and talk to God like I knew Him and He knew me. The selfish yearnings that had haunted me were replaced with a new desire to live for the One who had given Himself for me. Jesus said in John 15:16 **"You did not choose Me, but I chose you and appointed you, that you should go and bear fruit, and that your fruit should remain, that whatever you ask of the Father in My name, He may give to you."** It was as though I had just come to life; I was alive spiritually.

I can't say that my circumstances improved; as a matter of fact, they got worse. However, my response to my circumstances got better. Now I had hope and I learned to depend on God and trust Him for everything. As I faced life knowing that He was in control, that made all the difference in the world.

In spite of the changes inside me, Darren and I did separate and the problems with the kids got worse. We had tried all kinds of counseling with them and for our marriage as well. As I tried to get my priorities right with my husband before my kids, I found that I was still looking for their love and approval. We tried to maintain some sort of normalcy to our lives, even as the kid's behavior became more and more rebellious.

After several months with little progress, we found out about a Bible Study class on marriage that was starting at our church. I signed up immediately even though Darren still didn't want to have anything to do with it. We separated for the second time, this time Darren moved out and I was forced to just pray for God to work in our marriage. God's answer was not what I thought it would be. Isaiah 55:8-9 says, **"For My thoughts are not your thoughts, neither are your ways My ways, declares the LORD. For as the heavens are higher than the earth, so are my ways higher than your ways, and My thoughts than your thoughts."** When the marriage class was about to start and Darren was still refusing to go, I was still praying. When he finally told his sister that he would go, he said, "If this class makes me want to get back together with Cindy, I'm going to be so mad!" Well, we both went and God did begin to work in our lives and our marriage. As I began to learn the role of a wife and God's design for the marriage covenant, it was life changing for me. In the study of Genesis, I began to understand why and how we were created and how we were to live. This was a new beginning for me as a "baby Christian." Within a couple of weeks Darren moved back home. We wanted to try to work things out, and we committed to start over.

About three weeks into the Bible study, we were faced with a situation that would change the course of our lives forever. One Saturday night around midnight we got a phone call from the police. My daughter was in trouble. She was with some older kids who had been drinking and the police officer suggested I come and get her. The ride home was like a bad dream. She was crying hysterically, and I was very angry. She started saying that she wanted to kill herself, which really scared me. I didn't know what to do and was afraid to leave her alone. After getting a referral from the counselor we had been seeing, we admitted Carmen to a long-term treatment facility for teenagers.

That was an extremely emotional day. I was afraid this would be the last straw for our marriage. It seemed like things were just starting to turn around and now this! I was so confused. Why was this happening? I was about to learn the real meaning of Romans 8:28 **"And we know that God causes all things to work together for good to those who love God, to those who are called according to His purpose."**

God led us to a program for Carmen that was "a family education" program. While we could have no contact with our daughter for two months, we were required to attend classes about substance abuse and parenting twice a week. We didn't even realize that she had a drug problem when we admitted her. The program consisted of five phases that required the parents and children to be equally involved. In Carmen's second phase, we opened our home to host anywhere from four to six of the kids in the program overnight Sunday through Thursday. As we and the kids learned some extremely valuable "tools for change," we applied them to ourselves and held the kids accountable.

It was at this time that the lingering guilt from my abortions surfaced. I had never really talked to anyone about my abortions and had even lied to doctors when they asked how many times I had been pregnant. Even though I had confessed my sins to God and had turned my life over to Him, it was difficult to face my feelings of guilt and shame from the abortions. The hardest struggle was to see how God could forgive me, when I realized what I had actually done. Before I became a believer, I could rationalize my actions away. I could convince myself that what I had done was not really murder.

But now my conscience was trained by God's Word. I now had the Holy Spirit in me and I couldn't believe the lie anymore. I first had to ask God to forgive me and then I had the hard task of accepting His forgiveness. My pride resisted the truth that I had committed murder and then the truth that God forgives the sin of murder. When I realized that I truly did not deserve God's forgiveness, I finally began to understand the true meaning of the New Covenant. **"But He having offered one sacrifice for sins for all time, sat down at the right hand of God...for by one offering He has perfected for all time those who are sanctified...This is the covenant that I will make with them, after those days, says the Lord: I will put My laws upon their heart, and upon their mind I will write them... and their sins and their lawless deeds I will remember no more" (Hebrews 10:12-17).**

This healing process was very painful, but also very freeing. I learned that I often used anger to cover up my feelings of guilt, shame, hurt, and fear. It was also during this time that I acknowledged I was still sinfully using alcohol and drugs. As I recognized my contribution to the problems we were having with the kids in their rebellion, I had to stop blaming everyone else, look at myself, and accept responsibility for my behavior. With my faith in God, the knowledge of His Word and the work of God's Spirit in my heart, I began to understand what a healthy "normal" life was like as a "new creation" in Christ.

One Sunday, a few years later, I heard a sermon titled "The Sanctity of Life." The pastor showed us from the Bible that when David's infant son died, David was comforted in knowing that he would see his son again in heaven. He concluded that those who have had abortions can be forgiven of their sin and can anticipate being reunited with their child in heaven. Hearing this released years of pent up emotion; I started weeping. Never before had I heard anything so comforting. I was so uplifted that for the first time, I began to live in God's forgiveness and to stop dwelling on the past. This gave me renewed hope for the future.

In studying God's Word, I have learned about His character and His attributes. Through His love and forgiveness, He will heal all of our hurts if we are willing to humbly acknowledge our sin and ask Him for forgiveness. It is hard to face our desperate need, and we have to be willing to work at change. But God is always faithful to answer our prayers and to fulfill His promises.

Living in the Light of God's forgiveness made me realize that there were many people I had hurt because of my abortions. In God's timing and as He gave me opportunity, I wanted to seek forgiveness from those people. I also wanted to tell my daughter about my abortions and ask her forgiveness for the many hurts I had inflicted on her. She had so many questions about things that she didn't understand. I remember her asking, "How could you do that, Mom? What if it had been me?" That was hard to consider, but I had to trust God for wisdom and thank Him for her. I had often asked myself the same questions. I had believed the lie of the world; that it is my body and therefore my choice. Ephesians 4:17-18 says that before I gave my life to God I walked in the futility of my mind, being darkened in my understanding, excluded from the life of God because of my ignorance and the hardness of my heart. I could only take my daughter to God's Word for answers, the same answers He had given to me. Satan, the Father of lies, wants us to keep secrets and to tell lies. However, Jesus is the Way and the Truth and the Life, and when we turn our lives over to Him, His truth sets us free. The truth of God's forgiveness sets us free from the bondage of our sin. As a mother, it was hard to admit my sin, but God has used that to strengthen my relationship with my daughter.

Even though I still have unanswered "why" questions, I have come to rest in His sovereignty and have **"the peace of God, which surpasses all comprehension" Philippians 4:7a.**

As I have grown in His Word, He continues to give me strength and hope in knowing my past is forgiven and my future is certain. My life has changed in so many ways because of God and His grace. He has restored my marriage; He has healed all my hurts from the past; and He has given me a second chance in so many ways. Now I have the privilege of teaching other women God's Word through Bible Studies and living for Him every day. I am continually amazed at how God can use someone as lost as I was for His glory.

My prayer is that my story will be used for His purpose and in whatever way He chooses. I want to encourage you to surrender your life to Him. No matter what you have done in the past, if you will confess your sins, **"He is faithful and righteous to forgive us our sins and to cleanse us from all unrighteousness" (1 John 1:9).**

As I experienced God's forgiveness and grieved for my aborted babies, God's comfort encouraged me to write the words to this poem. May God bless you, and remember that God promises that when **"you call upon Me and come and pray to Me, and I will listen to you. And you will seek Me and find Me, when you search for Me with all your heart" (Jeremiah 29:12-13).**

Precious Children
By Cindy Yager

My precious little children,
So dear to my heart,
So close to me in spirit,
Yet so far apart.

Although I've never seen you,
I long to meet you face to face.
And when I stand before Him,
I know I will, by His sovereign grace.

Even though I know now
That you are safe and in His arms,
It grieves my heart when I think,
That in my sin I caused such harm.

My heart was weak and broken,
Because of my guilt and shame,
But now I rejoice in victory,
Because He chose me, to call upon His name.

He answered me in love,
And washed me clean forever.
Now my life has changed,
And will never be the same, not ever.

He wiped away my tears,
He took away my fears.
He is my hope and my story,
And to Him I give all the glory.

I have so many questions,
And things I want to know.
And as I draw closer to Him,
I just continue to grow.

I'm so thankful that by His grace and mercy,
I am now set free.
And I look forward to that day when I meet you,
And enter with you into eternity.

Cindy's Update:
Darren and Cindy live in Salt Lake City, Utah with their two girls. They attend an Evangelical Free Church where Darren serves on the elder board and Cindy teaches ladies' Bible Study. They both love the Lord and desire to serve Him in whatever way He asks of them. Cindy's daughter lives in Seattle with her husband and three small children. She recently celebrated her seventh year of sobriety and also has a deep desire to serve God and study His Word. God has restored Darren and Cindy's marriage and continues to draw them closer to Him as they share their experiences and hope with others.

Personally to you...
1. How were you encouraged after reading Cindy's story?

2. At what point(s) did you identify with her story?

3. Below are a few Scripture passages Cindy used. Which one(s) could you apply to your circumstance(s)? How do they help you?

• Romans 10:9

• Ezekiel 36:25-26

• Jeremiah 29: 12-13

Day 5

I don't know about you, but I could relate to each story in one way or another. Many times reading stories like these will bring back your painful memories. I pray that you found comfort in realizing that God was at work in each life. He is also at work in your life drawing you to Himself for the forgiveness and comfort His mercy and grace offer.

I want you to know how precious it is to me that you have come to the point of dealing with the abortion issues in your life. If you have had an abortion, God is ready to meet you on each page of this book to open the eyes of your heart so that you may begin to live in His forgiveness and find restoration of your soul. Please know that my prayers are continually with you as you seek the truth of God's Word.

As you go to the next chapter, I would like to ask if you are prepared to allow God's truth to penetrate your heart? Are you ready to allow God's forgiveness to heal the wounds of your sin? I know, without a doubt, that His love can penetrate your broken heart as you embrace Him with your open wounds.

Write out a prayer from your heart:

Chapter 2

"Then I will sprinkle clean water on you,
and you will be clean;
I will cleanse you from all your filthiness and from all your idols."
Ezekiel 36:25

Forgiveness Through Repentance

Day 6

Forgiveness Through Repentance

You have just read three precious stories of people that tell how each was affected by their choice to have an abortion. In all three cases, that decision compelled each one to face their desperate need for a Savior to relieve the guilt and shame of their sin. For Amy to face her need took acknowledging her responsibility for her abortions, recognizing how she had made a mess of her life, and turning to God who loved her despite the heinousness of her sin. In Cindy's life, it took the near break-up of her marriage for her to admit her need. She cried out, "I can't do it anymore." In Eddie's life it took much tragedy and seeing how his pastor faced tragedy to see his need for a Savior.

Even though you may be involved in a church, you may not be aware of how desperately each of us needs a Savior. Every one of us is deserving of death as the just punishment for our sins (Romans 3:23; 6:23). Only God is holy; God never sinned; only God could die for someone else's sin, and so He did. By becoming a man, God in the person of Jesus Christ paid the penalty for the sins of all those who recognize their desperate need and call upon Him for His mercy and His forgiveness. God does not call us to a religion, but He does call us into a love relationship through His Son, Jesus Christ, who paid the price for our sins (I Peter 3:18; Romans 5:6, 8). God has initiated this love relationship and demonstrated His love for us by dying in our place (Romans 5:8). The only reasonable response to such sacrificial love is to be devoted to Him, love Him, and obey what His Word says to do. The Bible says, **"And there is salvation in no one else; for there is no other name under heaven given among men, by which we must be saved" (Acts 4:12).**

You may be thinking, *"I am a good person; I am better than most people I know; I know God will give me credit for all the good things I have done."* But no amount of good can take away the guilt and shame for the sins you have committed. The Bible says in Romans 3:23 that we all fall short of God's standard and that **"There is none righteous, not even one" (Romans 3:10).**

Let's take a look at where it all began in the book of Genesis and see the first woman who was deceived into believing that what she was doing was right. Let's look at the story of Adam and Eve. In studying this passage, there is much we can glean as post-abortive women by looking at Eve and what she wanted. This account in Genesis will help you understand how your desires make you susceptible to the deceptiveness of sinful choices.

The Creator's Command

Read Genesis Chapters 2 and 3 in one sitting.
1. In Genesis 2:9, what two specific trees were in the garden?

   a.

   b.

2. Re-read Genesis 2:15-17. What command did God give to Adam in verse 17 and what was the consequence for disobeying that command?

   Command:

   Consequence:

3. What did God do for Adam in Genesis 2:18? Why did He do it?

4. Because Adam and Eve had not sinned, they were in total communion with God who is pure and holy. It says in Genesis 2:25 that they were both _____ and not _____. What is the cause of shame?

5. What do you learn about God from Genesis 2?

His power?

His authority?

His care for His creation?

His standard for human behavior?

His judgment for sin (disobedience)?

The Creator Questioned

1. Picture the scene in Genesis 3:1-3. Compare what Eve told the serpent that God said with what God actually said. Genesis 2:16-17; 3:2-3

What did Eve add?

Why was that wrong?

What was the consequence for eating the forbidden fruit?

2. Read Genesis 3:4-7. What lies did the serpent tell Eve?

Vs. 4: You shall surely not _____.

Vs. 5: Your _____will be opened, and you will be like

_____, knowing _____ and _____.

3. From verse 6, what made Satan's lies believable? How did Eve rationalize her decision to eat the fruit? Whom did she choose to believe?

Many women today have been deceived by the lies about abortion. The lie that the fetus is only unwanted tissue to be disposed of goes counter to God's involvement in forming life in the mother's womb. Read Psalm 139:13-16. The lie keeps women from seeing abortion as going against what God has ordained. Women are told they have the right to choose. Who gives them that right? The Bible says that God, our creator, is the giver of life and He determines how many days are ordained for each person.

What lies did you believe "would take care of your problem" at the time of your abortion? How did believing those lies deceive you when you chose to violate a right that belongs only to God? Read Deuteronomy 32:39 and describe the right that belongs to God alone.

4. Why do you think Adam also ate the fruit? Did he know it was wrong? What relationship did it violate and what relationship did it keep? (Isaiah 59:2) How did Adam's desire for human companionship affect his choice to disobey God?

5. Read James 1:14-15. What were Eve's desires or lusts that led her to sin against God's command? As you look back to the time of your abortion, what did you desire that enticed you to disobey God's command?

6. Write a brief definition of sin using James 1:14-15, Romans 3:23, 8:7.

Day 7

Consequences of Disobeying the Creator

Read Genesis 3:8-13.
1. What did Adam and Eve fear when they heard God call to them in the garden?

2. List 4 reasons why it is wise to fear God, and describe them here:

   Proverbs 3:12

   Proverbs 9:10

   Matthew 10:28

   Roman 6:23

So the wise person who fears the Lord will seek to be holy and keep her heart pure. 2 Corinthians 7:1 says, **"...beloved, let us cleanse ourselves of all defilement of flesh and spirit, perfecting holiness in the fear of God."** Holiness means to be set apart for God by keeping His commands. Adam and Eve's sin separated them from God and His holiness.

3. In what way are Adam and Eve, and all sinners since them, accountable to God for their sin? (Hebrews 9:27; Romans 14:12).

4. What did Adam do that made his guilt obvious in verse 10? How does this illustrate his and our exposure before an all-knowing God? Is there anywhere we can hide from God? (Psalm 139:7-12).

5. Since God knows everything, what is the result of hiding one's sin? (Psalm 32:3-4; Proverbs 28:13).

All sin has consequences, whether we acknowledge it or not. How can you relate to the suffering the Psalmist described in Psalm 32? What mental torment due to your guilt and shame have you experienced since your abortion?

Guilt and shame are part of the natural consequences to a conscience that has been exposed to God's law. What are your thoughts on Romans 7:7? Over time unresolved guilt and shame can lead to depression.

Ezra 9:6 expresses the guilt and shame the post-abortive woman feels. It says, "**...and I said, I am ashamed and embarrassed to lift up my face to Thee, my God, for our iniquities have risen about our heads, and our guilt has grown even to the heavens.**"

When the post-abortive woman struggles with guilt, she is really responding to two accusations from her conscience. First, she has aborted her child and secondly she has overruled her mothering instincts to care for her child. God has given us a conscience in order that we might experience guilt to drive us to repentance and salvation. (Read 2 Corinthians 7: 9-10). The truly repentant heart can then experience the joy of no longer living under the condemnation of their sin. (Read Romans 8:1). When accusations or depression return to your mind after repentance, the post-abortive woman must be fortified with God's promise of "no condemnation." It will take time and diligence to replace the old ways of thinking about your abortion with the reality of God's mercy. Memorize Romans 8:1 and any other verses that help you combat your old patterns of thinking such as:

- Psalm 55:22:   **"Cast your burden upon the Lord, and He will sustain you."**
- Psalm 126:5:   **"Those who sow in tears shall reap with joyful shouting."**
- Galatians 5:1:   **"It was for freedom that Christ set us free."**

6. How did Adam and Eve try to avoid taking responsibility for their sin in verses 12 and 13? Look at Genesis 3:16-19 to see if God held them both responsible for their sin.

One of the hardest things for post-abortive women is to have other people know about our sin. We, as post abortive women, attempt to shift the blame, to hide our sin, and to make excuses. Just like Adam, we are attempting to maintain an untainted image and avoid responsibility. First of all, pride is sin against a Holy God. It also affects our relationship with others. Have you seen how pride has affected the honesty in your relationships?

7. How do you think blaming Eve for his sin affected their marriage? What would Adam need to do to restore his relationship with both God and Eve? Write out Proverbs 28:13.

Read Genesis 3:15.

Commentators tell us that this is the first reference to the good news of God's plan and remedy for the consequence of sin. The woman's seed (Christ) would deal the serpent's seed (Satan) a fatal blow on the head by defeating death, the wage for sin, on the Cross. Christ was wounded on the heel only to rise again from death. PENALTY PAID!

Read Genesis 3:14-21

1. What were the immediate consequences of sin for the serpent? For Eve? For Adam?

2. What was the ultimate promised consequence (wage) for sin? (Genesis 2:17; 3:3; Romans 6:23).

3. Adam and Eve were spiritually alive in relationship to God prior to sin. They died to that relationship, yet did not immediately die physically. What kind of death is characterized by separation from God? (Romans 5:12, 18; Ephesians 2:1, 2).

4. In Genesis 3:21, what did God put to death to provide a covering for Adam and Eve now that they were sinners?

The Old Testament sacrificial system demonstrated God's requirement of a blood sacrifice as a covering for sin. That pointed to the sacrifice of God's Son on the Cross as the one death that covers all sin for all who place their trust in Him.

Because of God's great love for us, He provided a way for us to be restored to a right relationship with Him. We will look at that next. Be encouraged, my friend, God has prepared every step of the way to a right relationship with Him.

Day 8

I remember my dad telling my sister and me that if we ever got pregnant, we would have our babies. He was adamantly against abortion because the doctor had encouraged my parents to abort me at six months when my mom came down with Red Measles. The doctor assured my parents that I would be deformed, but my dad said they could not take my life. I thank the Lord that He preserved my life through my dad's firm stand against abortion. So although I was sexually active, I didn't want to disappoint my parents and I tried to be as "safe" as possible.

When I heard the gospel at age 19, I embraced Christ as my Savior and was immediately convicted of my sexual sin. I told the boy I was dating that we should not see each other any more. A month later, I found out I was pregnant. I went to my mom and my sister because I knew they would support what I thought I wanted. I did not want to ruin my reputation or embarrass my parents. I believed that abortion was my only choice and made an appointment at an abortion clinic. The day came. My sister went with me and waited outside because the clinic assured us that it would be a quick procedure.

While in the waiting room, I saw a girl who was probably six months pregnant. God convicted my heart that her baby was just like the one I carried in my body. I kept trying to deny the truth; I wanted to believe that mine was only a blob of tissue as I had heard in school. When the doctor came in to examine me, he saw that I was very nervous. He left telling the nurse that if I did not calm down, he was not going to continue. I convinced the nurse that I was fine and she then called for the doctor to return.

When the abortion procedure was over, they led me to a cot to recuperate. I could not quit crying. I remember the nurse saying, "Those must be tears of joy." I told her, "They are tears of much sorrow." I knew I had made a terrible mistake. The only thing I could think of at that moment was my dad telling me that this would never take place. As much as I wanted to believe that abortion took care of my problem, I sensed even then that my abortion would affect my whole life. I am here to tell you that it has. Just like Eve, I deceived myself into thinking that disobedience was the right thing. It wasn't just that I had disobeyed my dad. You see, even though I knew the civil law allowed abortion, and even though I told myself that I had a right to choose what to do with my body, deep down I knew that what I had done was wrong.

I remember facing my sister when it was over. Both of us were very ashamed and felt extremely guilty. I know that if there were one day in my sister's life that she would like to change, it would be that day. We both knew we had disobeyed our dad. The Bible says in Ephesians 6:1, **"Children, obey your parents in the Lord, for this is right."**

That hot July day God gave me three ways out. First, I knew the standard my daddy had set before me. Second, the pregnant girl in the waiting room was God's warning to me that I was about to take the life of my baby. Third, I became very nervous and the doctor's leaving the room could have been my "way of escape." For many years I grieved over compounding the sin of my abortion by not heeding these warnings. I Corinthians 10:13 promises that **"No temptation has overtaken you, but such as is common to man; and God is faithful, who will not allow you to be tempted beyond what you are able, but with the temptation will provide a way of escape also, that you may be able to endure it."**

What about you?
Are you seeing how your desires have led you to sin? List the practical "ways out" God gave you at the time of your abortion(s)? (Read I Corinthians 10:13 in the paragraph above.)

In what ways have you been hiding from God as Adam and Eve? Are you afraid to let people know about your abortion(s)? What have you done to hide it? From whom? How has that affected your relationship with God?

Your family?

Your marriage? If you have not told your husband, what does that say about the honesty in your relationship?

Take some time now and write down the lies you have believed about your abortion(s); your body; the baby you carried. Ask God how you have been deceived and what have you been trying to block out of your mind. Get alone with God and be honest with yourself and God.

Day 9

In 2 Samuel 11 and 12 we can read the story of David, the king of Israel, who paid a tremendous price for indulging his desires. He gave in to temptation for the beautiful Bathsheba bathing on her rooftop. He sent for her even though he knew she was married to a soldier who was fighting in his army. When Bathsheba became pregnant he tried to cover up their sin by bringing her husband home from the battlefield. The baby could then be considered her husband's and their sin would not be exposed.

David had not anticipated the character of Bathsheba's husband, Uriah. Uriah refused to go to his home while his comrades were still at war. David then resorted to greater lengths to cover their sin. Turn to 2 Samuel 11:14-15 to see what extreme measures he would use to avoid being exposed.

1. Write out what he wrote in the letter (vs 15).

2. Once Uriah was dead David took Bathsheba as his wife and she bore him a son. Write out God's opinion of his actions in 2 Samuel 11:27.

3. When David was confronted with his sin against God, what was his first response? (2 Samuel 12:13a).

4. As soon as David acknowledged his sin and confessed it, what were the prophet's words to him? (vs 13b).

5. What were the consequences of David's sin even though God forgave him? (vs 14).

6. When the child became sick David fasted and prayed that God would let the child live. He received a "no answer" to his prayer. Read his response to the news that the child had died and give the reason for his change in behavior. (2 Samuel 12:20-23).

7. What was the confidence that David expressed in Verse 23 and what was the basis of his response?

Although David's sin was heinous in God's sight, God forgave him immediately and David was confident that he would spend eternity with God and that his child would also be there. We have seen how quickly David took responsibility for his sin, and it is important for the post-abortive woman to recognize her responsibly before God. David's sin compounded from the time he gave in to his original desires and committed adultery through his attempts to cover up his sin. The post-abortive woman must be willing to face her responsibility for her sin from the point of conception through the ensuing years of cover up.

Think through the entire process to recognize and confess to God where you have violated God's commands for your life.

8. How have you violated what God says about sexual sin? (Hebrews 13:4; I Thessalonians 4:3-6).

9. When you found out you were pregnant what options did you consider? Who did you consult? Why did you consult them? What carried the most weight in your decision? What clues came to your mind that it was wrong? How did you violate what God says? (Deuteronomy 32:39; Exodus 20:13).

10. On the day of your abortion, who drove you there? Who went with you? What kind of information did you receive from the staff? Did you see any ways of escape as it talks about in I Corinthians 10:13

11. After the euphoria of solving the problem, when did you begin to sense guilt and shame? To what extent have you tried to cover up your guilt and shame? How has deception become a way of life for you? How does this violate what God says? (Proverbs 12:22; 19:9; Ephesians 4:25)

God requires us to be honest in our relationships with others, and the closer the relationship the more we reveal about ourselves. It is not necessary to tell everyone about your abortion, but it is important that you be honest with close family members, particularly your husband. Godly counsel and prayer should precede communicating with them.

Let's take a look at the provision God has made for your sins to be forgiven, including your sin of abortion. Can you even imagine how very much God loves you to provide Himself in payment for your sins when you have gone against His clear command not to take a life? (Romans 5:8-9).

Day 10

God's Answer For Sin

Read John 3:16-21

1. What motivated God to become a man? (vs 16).

2. What did God want to help people avoid? (vs 16).

3. What does it mean to perish if a person does not believe? (vs 16; Hebrews 9:27).

4. What did God send His Son into the world to do? What was NOT His purpose? (vs 17).

5. Why are all men condemned already without Christ? (vs 18; Romans 3:23).

6. Unless one has come to the light (been born again), what does he practice? (vs 19). How does God view His deeds?

7. Why do people want to avoid the "light" of God's truth? (vs 20). What does someone in the dark fear according to verse 20?

8. When a person comes to the light, what does he practice? What will others see in his life? (vs 21).

To bridge the gap sin brought between God and man, God's love provided forgiveness through His sinless Son. Jesus paid the price of death on the cross for the sins of the world. Because the debt for sin has been paid God offers forgiveness to those who turn from their sin and accept Jesus' payment for their sin. (Ephesians 2:8-9).

Apart from Jesus Christ, no one can ever be forgiven for their abortion(s). Jesus as God is the only one who could have died for sin because He had no sin of His own. Take a minute to look up these scriptures. What do these verses say about Jesus?

Acts 4:12

Romans 10:9-10

A person who comes to Jesus for forgiveness must acknowledge her sin and turn from that sin. She must realize her own helplessness to make up for what she has done. She must call on God in the same desperate and trusting way a drowning person calls on a lifeguard to rescue him.
Read the following verses:

Ephesians 2:8-9

Titus 3:5

What can "you do" to be saved?

Can all of your best efforts cancel the debt for your sin of abortion?

When a person acknowledges her sin, she is brokenhearted over her sin against a Holy God, and purposes to turn from her sinful lifestyle to live by God's standards. Placing her faith in Christ's payment for her sin on the Cross, her repentant heart is ready to receive God's gift. Repentance is a turning, a change of heart and mind from going one's own sinful way to embrace God's forgiveness and follow His direction through His Word. When a person repents, she turns from her sin and by faith she turns to Christ.

In the New Testament we see the heart of Jesus toward one sinful woman, who was actually caught in the very act of adultery.

Read John 8:1-11.

1. Try to put yourself in the place of the woman in this scene. Describe how she must have been feeling. How would you feel in front of Jesus right after your abortion(s)? Describe those feelings below. What circumstances have brought you face to face with Jesus? (vs 3-5).

2. She was only a pawn. What were her accusers trying to accomplish with their cruel treatment of her? (vs 6).

3. With all eyes focused on this poor woman, how did Jesus' stooping down draw the attention of the crowd away from her? (vs 6b).

4. What did Jesus make the Pharisees see so that they left her alone with Him? (vs 7).

5. How did Jesus' words and actions display these characteristics of His Deity?

Compassion (Psalm 103:12-14)

Wisdom (Job 9:4)

Justice (Isaiah 45:21)

Mercy (Micah 7:18-19)

6. How does Jesus' character and His treatment of this woman give you hope?

7. How did the exposure of her sin turn out to be a good thing?

Have you ever thought that exposing your sin of abortion could bring God's blessing to your life? What is the most important thing to you: your obedience or your reputation? (Circle one)

Day 11

I remember the day I became a Christian. Everything changed! On July 14, 1978, I was nineteen and sitting in a small country church in Gastonia, North Carolina. When God opened my eyes to see myself as a sinner on the world's broad road that leads to destruction (Matthew 7:13-14), I was broken and sought God's forgiveness for my sin. God forgave me and put me on the narrow path - a path of life and abundance (John 10:9-10). I had found the answer to the nagging question in my mind: "Isn't there more to life than eating, sleeping, and working?" I saw the beauty in nature around me differently as I walked out of the church that day. I was encouraged that there was real purpose for living.

My prayer for you is that you will ask the Lord Jesus to be the Lord and Savior of your life - that you will seek His Kingdom and His righteousness first so that you may find all your needs met in Him (Matthew 6:33). There is no lasting peace or joy apart from Him. Today, if you recognize your hopeless and helpless condition, will you take time now to call upon the name of the Lord and be saved? (Romans10:9-13).

Your Response
As you have read this chapter and participated in this Bible Study, how is God prompting you to respond?

• Have you changed anything you believe about God? Your rights? Your body? Your responsibility before God?

• What is going on in your heart? Are you angry? Bitter? Repentant? What do you need to do to make any necessary changes?

- Have you acknowledged your sin against a holy God?

- Have you turned from your sinful lifestyle and embraced God's standards for your life?

- Have you placed your faith in Christ's payment for your sin?

- What steps will you take to change and what can you do to begin today?

As you turn to the next chapter you will read two wonderful stories of how God's forgiveness and reconciliation brought each of these women closer to God. I will be sharing how God worked in my own life to reconcile my family after 17 years of hiding my abortion from my Dad. Our God is an amazing God. He truly cares about every detail of our lives (Philippians 1:6). He cares deeply for you and has provided all you need to know Him and to live wisely in this world (2 Peter 1:3-5).

Chapter 3

"For if you forgive men for their transgressions,
your heavenly Father will also forgive you."
Matthew 6:14

Clearing the Conscience

Day 12

Nobody Told Me
By Cynthia Fong

When I was in the eighth grade, I was asked if I wanted to accept Christ as my personal Savior. My immediate response was, "yes." But my answer was given without any understanding of what that decision would require of me. I had no idea that He was to be the Lord of every part of me, that every part of my life was to be lived in obedience to Him. I didn't understand what it meant to follow Him. To this day, I do not believe that I became a Christian at that time, but I did begin to participate in Christian activities - attending Friday night fellowship and Sunday morning church. The rest of the week, however, was under my own direction. I lived my life just as I pleased.

Relationships with men presented the greatest obstacle to me in living a life pleasing to God. Those I dated were not the kind of men Christ would have for me. I was attracted to the excitement of "bad boys" - many of whom were emotionally abusive, drug users, divorced, alcoholics, or cheaters. These "bad boys," had one thing in common: they all rejected Christianity.

It is overwhelming to me now to know that while I pursued my selfish desires, God protected me from contracting a sexually transmitted disease that could have cost me my life. Recently, the emotional agony of awaiting test results reminded me of the truth that promiscuous relationships were never worth the pain that I experienced - then or now.

Two relationships stand out as having particularly devastating impacts on my life. First was "Randy," whom I met and dated when I was only 16. He had a way of making me feel special, and sweeping me off my feet with his smooth-talk. A non-believer with no interest in spiritual things, Randy was reluctant to go to church with me. I was the one who conceded; I gave up going to church in order to be with him. Rationalizing that choice was easy. I simply convinced myself that I was going to "win him to Christ." As a result, my compromise made him only more interested in me - not God.

Almost immediately, our relationship began to change. As our involvement with each other escalated, Randy made it clear that he wanted a more physical relationship. I felt torn. I was afraid of losing him and afraid of losing what I had been told was my most precious gift: my virginity. But a decision not to back off is a decision to move forward. When we were together one day, we crossed the line. I tried to put the reins on our over-involvement by saying, "no," but he wasn't listening anymore. Then it was over. All I remember are the tears. I cried for a long time. I was so remorseful over my failed testimony, my broken relationship with God, the loss of my virginity, and the disillusionment of a physical relationship out of wedlock. I was totally heartbroken.

Even after that, I was not ready to give up on relationships with the wrong guys, because I longed to be loved. Relationships came and went as I sought to fill my longing for love, yet trying to avoid hurt at all cost. The pattern that developed was destructive. At the time, I could not see how using others and allowing myself to be used in this way was sinful and harmful both spiritually and emotionally.

Then I met "Steve." When he came into my life, it was as though the man of my dreams swept into my life and I was certain that everything was changing for the better. In so many ways, he seemed to be my "knight in shining armor." He possessed every quality I wanted. He was a growing Christian; he was good with kids; he could cook; and he even spoke Cantonese, which was important in my family. When I met him, I was certain that my prayers had been answered.

As we continued to date, our relationship became more intense and physical. We both knew that sex before marriage was wrong biblically and morally. (Hebrews 4:12) It was easy to say to each other that we were going to stop being physically intimate, but it was much harder to do it. Being accountable only to each other was no good when we were enjoying how good it felt to be together. In our shame, we kept our sin a secret, unwilling to share our weakness with other brothers and sisters in Christ and to seek the accountability we so desperately needed. Before long, we convinced each other that it was all right to have sex since we were talking about marriage in the near future. Always careful to practice birth control, Steve and I attempted to enjoy the pleasures of sin while avoiding the consequences. But we only fooled ourselves.

Everything seemed perfect. I had just graduated from college. Graduate school was beginning and I was with the man I loved and wanted to be with for the rest of my life. Then came the day I missed my period. "Sometimes that happens," I thought to myself. Shortly thereafter I began to get sick, as if I had stomach flu. I figured it was just something that was "going around" in the classroom where I had begun my new teaching job. After two months, I still hadn't had a period. Steve and I began to worry. Finally, we purchased a home pregnancy test. The results were positive.

"How could this happen?" I thought to myself. "We used protection most of the time." I didn't want to talk to Steve or anyone else about being pregnant, denying the obvious. But hard as I wished, it wouldn't go away. In my desperation, I even tried to do things to cause a miscarriage, but failed. Nothing seemed to resolve my very real, very frightening dilemma.

At last I came to accept the fact that I was really pregnant. Steve and I talked about our choices. We were too afraid to tell our parents because we knew what their reaction would be: anger. Both of us grew up in traditional Chinese families where our parents constantly taught us not to get physically involved until marriage. In addition, we felt that having the baby at that time would affect both of our dreams of going to graduate school. It would be too hard to share our secret with friends. We felt ashamed and were afraid to have people at church learn of what we had done. Again, we made empty promises to each other to ease the pain. "We'll have children together in the future," we told one another. "There will be a better time." With that we decided to have an abortion.

Together we went to a clinic for an abortion. An ultrasound was performed by the nurse to determine how far along my pregnancy was. Results of the ultrasound showed that I was one day short of being four months pregnant. There wasn't much time. I was already too far along for the clinic to deal with "my problem" that day. I had to make an appointment for the following week. It was a long, hard week, one in which Steve and I managed to avoid the topic.

The next week, we went back to the clinic in the morning. The doctor inserted laminaria in me to dilate me, then instructed me to return in the afternoon. We went shopping to take our mind off things. When we returned, the nurse brought us into the room to check my vitals and to perform another ultrasound. When she left the room, Steve and I noticed that she left the picture of our "problem" on the ultrasound. There we saw hands and feet. What we saw was a baby. Both of us began to cry. When the nurse came back and found us crying, she asked Steve if I was okay. I remember the anger I felt at her insensitivity. I just wanted it over and convinced myself that it was too late to turn back. I proceeded with the abortion. As I look back now, I see how the Lord meant to use that ultrasound and my reaction to the insensitive nurse to prevent me from having the abortion. Even though He had offered me a clear way of escape, I chose to rebel.

My relationship with Steve began to change after the abortion. We had a hard time communicating with each other and we never talked about the abortion. Only two of our friends knew what we had done. We were no longer physically intimate; at times, he wouldn't even hug me. The memories of the abortion were eating me up inside. I began to realize that God was not a part of our relationship. Six months later, I broke off our relationship because I wanted it to be Christ-centered again. It was my hope that we would work on our individual walks with the Lord before getting back together. It hurt so much to break up with him because he had been my "knight in shining armor."

It wasn't long before Steve and I broke up for good. I moved to another city to begin graduate school. It was after that move that the memories of my abortion really began to affect me. I struggled with the reality that I had lost both my best friend and my baby. That's when I turned to God and cried out to Him for help and for salvation. I knew that He was there listening to me cry, standing beside me.

One particular weekend, when I came home from school, I was hurting for someone to talk to about my feelings. I remembered that my home church supported the Crisis Pregnancy Center (CPC). I found their telephone number and called. A counselor talked with me and I made an appointment to meet with her the very next day. That conversation led to my participation in the Center's post-abortion support group and, eventually, to my work as a volunteer at the Center. Through their post-abortion group study, I learned that I needed to seek forgiveness from God, my parents, and Steve. I confessed my sins to the Lord and asked for His forgiveness. I learned that **"If we confess our sins, He is faithful and just and will forgive us our sins and purify us from all unrighteousness" (1 John 1:9 - NIV).**

Next I went to my parents. I recall how upset my mother was that I had put myself at risk by having an abortion that could have caused me physical injury or threatened my life. I couldn't go to my father. I was so afraid of destroying the "Daddy's little girl" relationship that I cherished. It was my mother who broke the news to him. It grieved his heart to learn he had lost his first grandchild. Neither of my parents rejected me, but both were upset that I hadn't turned to them for help. Receiving their forgiveness was like a healing balm.

In the course of my recovery, I also realized the importance of forgiving the people in my life who had hurt me and seeking forgiveness for my sin against Steve. One year after our break up, I wrote Steve a letter, asking him to forgive me for all that I had done wrong in our relationship. It was a hard lesson, but I knew that I could not continue to blame him for all that had happened. I was there at the abortion clinic too. The decision to abort was mutual. Though he was not receptive to my letter, I knew I had done what was right before the Lord.

My last stop was a visit to the clinic where the abortion was performed. Going back there was the most difficult because I remembered everything, from sitting in the waiting room to seeing my ultrasound. That experience, gave me new understanding of Jesus' words, **"Forgive them, for they know not what they are doing" (Luke 23:24).** I praise the Lord that I was able to obtain the ultrasound image of my baby and have that one memory of him or her.

There is so much I have learned, that it is hard to remember just how little I understood at the time that the decision to take the life of my child would be life-changing. Why was I unwilling to think about the consequences? Nobody told me that having an abortion would affect the relationship I had with my boyfriend. Nobody told me that my abortion would hurt my parents far more than my being pregnant. Nobody told me that God saw and knew my unborn child, and that I would have to live with the consequences of knowing that my choice took a life. Nobody told me.

On the other hand, I had kept my secrets to myself. I chose not to tell anyone about how I was struggling with sexual purity in my thoughts and actions because I was too ashamed and too proud. Because I did not seek out biblical relationships of love and accountability, I chose the "quiet" way out. It seemed the best and easiest way. But there was no lasting relief in that decision. I was left with a lot of painful memories from my experience. Looking back, I wish I had thought to contact a place like CPC so I could have learned about my choices and about the consequences of those choices - beforehand.

Abortion is, by no means, the "easy way out." What follows are emotional, physical, relational, and spiritual consequences. The memories and emotions of my abortion are still with me and, on occasion, overwhelm me with feelings of guilt and regret. Mother's day, the day of my abortion, and the day of my due date are the hardest days of the year. It's hard not to indulge those feelings every once in a while and wonder "what if...?"

Even though I know that I can never change what I have done, I look to the Cross and remember daily that it was there that God made it possible to change everything. In 1 Corinthians 6:9-11 - NIV, we read, **"Do you not know that the wicked will not inherit the kingdom of God? Do not be deceived: Neither the sexually immoral, nor idolaters, nor adulterers, nor male prostitutes, nor homosexual offenders, nor thieves, nor the greedy, nor drunkards, nor slanderers, nor swindlers will inherit the kingdom of God. And that is what some of you were. But you were *washed,* you were *sanctified,* you were *justified* in the name of the Lord Jesus Christ and by the Spirit of our God"** (emphasis mine). I do not deserve to inherit the kingdom of God. I only deserve an eternity in hell. But because I have put my trust in Christ and His death on the Cross in my place, I am free from the guilt of my sin (Psalm 32:5).

For me, the most wonderful word in the 1 Corinthians passage is the word "But." That is where God changed everything. I deserve hell, <u>but</u> He cleansed me white as snow from my sins - *washed.* I deserve hell, but He set me apart and separated me from my sin - *sanctified.* I deserve hell, <u>but</u> He declared me "not guilty" before Him - *justified.* Because of Christ I am free from the bondage of my abortion. I am truly forgiven and set free by Him. Now I can be used to help others live in His forgiveness as I do.

Cynthia's Update:
Cynthia graduated with a MA degree in 2000 and then she went to Hong Kong to serve as a missionary at a place called Mother's Choice. She is currently working with the special needs children and

supervising the pregnant girls' services. She would also like to lead post abortion groups.

Personally to you...
1. How were you encouraged after reading Cynthia's story?

2. At what point(s) did you identify with her story

3. Below are a few Scripture passages Cynthia used. Which one(s) could you apply to your circumstance(s)? How do they help you?

• Hebrews 4:12

• 1 John 1:9

• 1 Corinthians 6:9-11

Day 13

His Perfect Will For My Shameful Life
Brenda Ownbey

My childhood was every child's dream. Ours was a middle-class family living in a small western town. Both my parents were loving and I adored my little brother. Early memories are of family outings: camping, fishing, and going to church together. When my mom thinks of me during those years, she describes me as loving to laugh, and to make others laugh as well. It was an idyllic time. But as we grow older, and the outside world invades our youthful reality, life changes, and not always for the better.

My life was changed in a single, tragic day. It was the summer between eighth grade and my freshman year of high school. I was 14 years old. I was home alone. My little brother was playing with a friend; Mom and Dad were both at work. We had some neighbors who had a sixteen-year-old son whom I liked secretly. I didn't know he had a dark side. On this particular day, this young man entered our house and did the unthinkable: he raped me. I didn't even fully understand what had happened to me. I was 14 years old and my life had been so sweet. What had just happened?

I recall the next day, as our family prepared to go on a trip together, I tried to tell my parents, but the words wouldn't come. I found myself unable to completely express to them the truth of what had happened. Maybe it was a sense of shame that kept me from telling the whole story. I felt tarnished. My innocence was gone and yet it remained unclear to me what the experience meant to my young life. Even afterwards, the boy and I spoke to each other. "Maybe," I thought, "this experience simply meant that we would eventually get married."

My first year of high school was a tough one. I felt as though there was something different about me and I wondered if anyone knew it or understood it. Was I normal? As a result, I pushed myself to get involved in a variety of school activities, yet never felt that I really fit in. Something wasn't right and I knew it.

My confusion would play itself out in a series of poor decisions that followed. At 16, and the new recipient of a driver's license, I took a girlfriend with me to "cruise the drag." That night a couple of young men waved us over and we stopped to talk to them. These guys were very nice looking. How exciting! Imagine our surprise when we discovered they were freshmen in college. Shortly thereafter, I began a relationship with one of those young men. I was thrilled to be dating an older guy. Unfortunately, ours progressed into a sexual relationship. Looking back, I believe I thought that having a sexual relationship with a man meant that he loved you. Not long after we became intimate, I discovered I was pregnant. I went to my boyfriend with this information and we talked about getting married and having the baby. There was, however, a problem. He was just starting in college and I was still in high school. Confused and frightened, I turned to my boyfriend for a solution. He told me he thought I should have an abortion.

The situation was no clearer to me after telling my mom the news. I had always wanted to be a wife and a mother and yet my own mother agreed that an abortion was the best and only option for me. It was she who made the appointment with our family gynecologist, also an abortionist.

As I sat waiting for my turn with the doctor, I wondered about the decision I was making - or had been made for me. Is this really the right thing to do? They put me to sleep for the procedure, so thankfully, I have no recollection of the event that took my baby's life. But I do remember being asked to leave through a different door, one that would not take me through the patient's waiting area. I sensed shame in the medical personnel there for their involvement in what happened in that office.

Even after enduring this experience, I continued the relationship with my college boyfriend. I did my best to not think about what had happened. When I was 19, we married. It was a marriage built on lies, fornication, and an abortion. It was a rocky place to start and it only got worse.

It was only a matter of time before I began to see an abusive side of my husband. He started going to bars and became physically and emotionally abusive to me. Instead of dealing with the problem, I threw myself into my career, working as much as 80 hours a week. Even though we were rarely together, our relationship continued to worsen. He was still going to school and I had a heavy work schedule. I was focused on finding fulfillment in my work. When we were together, there was usually a fight, which ended with my husband going to a local bar.

After three tumultuous years of marriage, we were tired of each other and our marriage. Around this time, I discovered from a co-worker that my husband was seeing another woman. One day after he came home from work, I decided to confront him about the matter. His reaction was violent. That night he beat me so badly that I began vomiting up blood. He left me to call my own ambulance. During my stay in the hospital, nurses would come in every half hour to ask me what had happened. I never told them the truth. As the evening wore on, I remember thinking, "Brenda, you cannot continue living like this."

I had never told my parents about the state of my marriage. For too long I kept hoping everything would, magically, change for the better. But that night, as I lay in the hospital, I decided to tell them. It was the middle of the night when they got my call. They promised to come and get me that weekend and they did. They packed my things and I moved home. My intention was never to get a divorce, but rather to try to heal our relationship. That was not my husband's perspective, however. He wanted out, and filed for divorce. For a year, I let devastation have its way with me. It was the hardest year of my life; I believed there was no hope for my life. "I am 23 years old," I kept reminding myself. "I've been raped, had an abortion, and divorced." I felt completely worthless. However, after that seemingly endless year, I decided to go back to school and earn a degree in social work.

Even this new distraction wouldn't keep the pain away. It was Christmas time when I drove to a hotel to end my life. At the hotel, I took 100 aspirin. Afterwards, lying on the bed, I remember thinking I didn't want to die, but that I had no other option. Then I was reminded of a family I had just recently met that was so different from any I had ever known. I felt compelled to call them. As a result, I was quickly taken to the nearest hospital. But now I had to face my parents. There was so much shame in that moment; I knew I could never again hurt them in that way. Still I wondered, if I lived, how would I find hope for my shameful life?

Christmas was not a happy time for our family that year. I remember sobbing in my father's arms, begging him to help me. But, he couldn't take away that deep hurt that I had harbored in my heart for so many years. Several days later I received a call from Bill, a man who was a friend of a co-worker of mine. My friend had tried to introduce the two of us on several occasions, but I had resisted, not yet ready to test the waters of a new relationship. Still he called. Of all evenings, he wanted to meet on New Year's Eve - the evening of new beginnings.

Though my heart wasn't in it, I decided it might be a good idea to go out for a little fun. He arrived to pick me up for our date. Our first discussion was about New Year's resolutions. It was at that moment that I looked at this new man in my life and thought, "I would really like to get closer to God." I had tried in my own way and realized that I had failed. What I didn't know was that this out-of-the-blue friendship was God's way of answering that prayer of my heart.

The friendship between Bill and myself was solidified over the next couple of months. I realized the many ways he was different from the man I had married. He was kind, gentle, and sensitive. The love I longed for was standing before me and I was gripped by fear. If he really knew me, would he want to keep seeing me? We had begun going to church together and I saw that he had a genuine love for the Bible. I couldn't hold my secret any longer. I decided to tell him about my past, believing that it would put an end to my feelings of hypocrisy - and probably the relationship, too.

I invited Bill to my parent's cabin, where I intended to lay out my whole sordid tale. Over supper, I began my story. In the course of that monologue, I realized I had never shared my past with any-one before. As my story unfolded, I began to cry and to shake. The reaction I received was just the opposite of what I expected. When I was done, Bill said with gentleness, "Brenda, one day you are going to blossom in the Lord and I want to be there." Three weeks after that day, I met with a Christian woman for lunch. She explained that I was a sinner and I was totally separated from God. As I saw my need to repent from my sinful, prideful way of life and turn to Christ, I cried and cried for God in His grace and mercy to save such a wretched sinner as I!!! Through the blood of Jesus as payment for my sin, God forgave me and gave me hope.

A year and a half later, Bill and I were married. God was start-ing a new chapter in my life - His chapter. As Psalm 103:3 promis-es, **"He forgives all my sins and heals all my diseases. He redeems my life from the pit and crowns me with love and compassion (NIV)."**

I wish I could say that was the end of all my hurt and that my life from that point on was perfect. But this was not the end of my story. After one year of marriage, I became pregnant. My husband and I were thrilled. In my twelfth week of pregnancy, I lost the baby. I remember again feeling the shame I had known before Christ entered my life. I began to think, I deserve to lose this baby and for God to punish me this way. I was overwrought with the belief that I was the source of heartache in our marriage and that Bill would have to share the pain of the consequences of my sin. Then blame made its way further into my thoughts as well. It became easy to focus blame on my mother since she was the one who had taken me to the doctor's office for the abortion. My bitterness, anger, and resentment toward her grew. As I allowed bitterness to take root in my heart, I began blaming her for other hurtful times in my life, including the day I was raped. Why wasn't she there when I needed her?

But God would not leave me in my despair. He proved Himself to be the Healer of even the strongest hurts. Two years after Bill and I were married, God led me to talk things out with my mother. We decided on a weekend. Bill made plans to be away, and Mom came for a visit. God got right to work. It was Saturday morning, over coffee, when God opened my heart and I confessed all the hurtful feelings I had harbored towards my mother. Tears and hugs followed. It was then that I asked my Mom for her forgiveness and she asked for mine. Since that day, God has restored our relationship and she has become my good friend.

I have experienced the power of God's Word in my life. I have memorized verses that remind me of His promise of forgiveness. Hebrews 10:17,18 says, "**...their sins and lawless acts I will remember no more. And where these have been forgiven, there is no longer any sacrifice for sin (NIV).**" Through hours of prayer and Bible study, God has brought me to understand that all my sins have been taken to the Cross. Isaiah 43:18 says, "**Forget the former things; do not dwell on the past**" **(NIV).** Again and again, God shows me that my abortion is forgiven and that it can and is being used for my good and the encouragement of others (Romans 8:28). Even when we think we are stumbling in darkness, God has a plan.

My message to those who have walked through the pain of abortion is this: do not continue to hang on to past sin. God is willing and able to release us from our burdens and set us free from hurt and shame. He delights in mending broken hearts. (Jeremiah

9:24) Be encouraged also that in our weakness, His strength is made known. I Corinthians 1:26-27 says, **"Brothers, think of what you were when you were called. Not many of you were wise by human standards; not many of you were influential; not many were of noble birth. But God chose the foolish things of the world to shame the wise, and God chose the weak things of the world to shame the strong" (NIV).** By God's grace, we can step out into the future He has planned for us, daring to allow Him to use every experience to glorify Him and to impact those He brings into our lives.

Brenda's UPDATE:
Bill and Brenda live in Salt Lake City, UT with three precious girls. Bill serves as the English Minister of the Salt Lake Chinese Church. Brenda spends much time home schooling their girls, discipling women in the Word, and being the wife of a pastor. God has blessed Brenda with such compassion for the needs of hurting women.

Personally to you...
1. How were you encouraged after reading Brenda's story?

2. How did you identify with her story?

3. Below are a few Scripture passages Brenda used. Which one(s) could you apply to your circumstance(s)? How do they help you?

   • Psalm 103:3

- Jeremiah 9:24

- I Corinthians 1:26-27

Day 14

Lets take the next few days to see how God hears the cries of His children. As you look up each verse, read each one several times and then rewrite the verse in your own words.

• Psalm 30:2-5

• Psalm 34:1-5 (Could you embrace verse 5?)

• Psalm 34:17-18

• Psalm 18:6

- Isaiah 41:10

- Psalm 145:18-19

- James 5:13-16

Take time to memorize one or more of these verses. Get a 3 x 5 index card (I like the bright colored ones!) and write the verse(s) on the card. Carry it with you wherever you go this week and review it several times daily. Be prepared to quote the verse to the ladies in your group if you are doing this study as a small group. Ponder what the verse teaches you about God.

Chapter 4

"And as for you, you meant evil against me,
but God meant it for good in order to bring about
this present result, to preserve many people alive."
Genesis 50:20

God's Principles for Living in Reconciliation

Day 15

Did you know that more Chapters in the Bible are written about the life of Joseph than any other human character in the Bible? God must have something to say to us through his life. Even though Joseph suffered at the hands of others, he grew strong by trusting God and being faithful. When life's difficulties are closing in on us, we can find hope, direction, and resolution on the pages of God's Word. I think you will see that the way Joseph handled his trials offers great insight for us as post-abortive women.

Read Genesis Chapters 37, 39-50 in one sitting.
1. List the ways Joseph was sinned against in chapters 37, 39, 40.

2. What did you see that Joseph did to bring trouble on himself? How do you identify with being sinned against and bringing trouble on yourself?

3. When we pick up Joseph's story in Genesis 39, Joseph has been stripped of his identity and sold as a slave in a foreign country. Who went with Joseph according to Genesis 39:2?

4. What fears do you think Joseph faced as he rode along in that caravan to Egypt?

5. What choices did Joseph have to make in order to experience God's presence and blessing? Deuteronomy 10:12-13; Psalm 56:3-4; Proverbs 3:5-6.

6. What assurance of God's presence with the believer is found in these verses? Psalm 139:7-12; Proverbs 15:3; Jeremiah 23:23-24; Hebrews 13:5.

God knows every detail of your life: your past, present and future. He even knows what is in your heart today. He is gracious and loving and always near to help you. Read Philippians 4:5. Describe any situations in your life that you wish God did not know.

What do you do to include God in your life? List ways you did not trust God when you were considering your abortion.

7. What do you think was going through Joseph's mind in Chapter 39 when he ended up in jail even after fleeing sexual temptation? What motivated Joseph to flee that temptation? (Vs. 9).

Joseph embraced the principle in 1 Corinthians 10:13 where God promises a way of escape when facing temptation. This all-important truth is one all believers should have with them at all times. Write 1 Corinthians 10:13 on a 3 x 5 card and put it where you will see it daily until it becomes the first thing you think of when you are tempted.

8. In verse 39:21 who was with Joseph in jail? What did the Lord do for Him? List ways God's presence has been evident in your life.

9. When things did not turn out as you thought they should, did you ever question God? What do these verses tell you about what God is doing in your life?

   Isaiah 55:8-9

   Jeremiah 29:11-13

   Roman 8:28-29

10. By the time Joseph had been in prison for a while, he must have been tempted to think that God had forgotten about him. Still he remained faithful, doing what was right. What does Genesis 41:38-39 say that Pharaoh and his servants saw in Joseph?

11. What evidence of the Spirit of God is obvious in your life? Can others see it? In what ways has God used your abortion experience to make you more like Christ?

12. Are you more interested in God and His Word since the pain of your experiences? What truths of God's Word have you embraced?

13. Since Joseph was faithful in each of the situations where he found himself, God continually gave him more responsibility. His blessing was related to his obedience. What were the privileges of Joseph's new position? (Genesis 41:40-45).

14. God's plan was bigger than just blessing Joseph for his obedience. God wanted to use Joseph to preserve His chosen people. God gave Joseph and his wife Asenath two sons. What did Joseph name his sons and how do those names reveal what was in Joseph's heart? (Genesis 41:51-52).

15. Their names show Joseph had hope. How can you tell he was not holding on to bitterness from the past? How do you think he was able to do this? (Genesis 45:5) Have you been able to do this? Read Joshua 1:5-9 and Hebrews 10:17-18. What things in your past are you bitter about?

We have seen how Joseph was obedient in circumstances that looked hopeless. As he trusted God and obeyed God, God blessed his life and increased his responsibility even though some of his circumstances did not change for the better. He was faithful in each situation. He is a great example for the post-abortive woman. His life demonstrates that we can obey God in any situation and trust Him for the outcome. As you look back you can see that your decision to abort your baby violated God's command. You probably did not believe God could bring good out of your situation. Even though you sinned in this way, God will forgive that sin and let you start afresh to live by His principles from this day forward. Tomorrow we will take a look at the character of God as we seek to obey Him and live a life that is honoring to Him.

Day 16

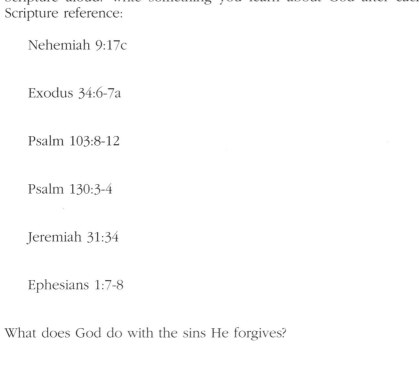

The following Scriptures will give you insight into God's character that will lead you to trust Him in order to obey Him. Read each Scripture aloud. Write something you learn about God after each Scripture reference:

Nehemiah 9:17c

Exodus 34:6-7a

Psalm 103:8-12

Psalm 130:3-4

Jeremiah 31:34

Ephesians 1:7-8

What does God do with the sins He forgives?

Do you think He will forgive the sin of abortion(s)?

Can He forgive and change your bitter heart? What must you do? (I John 1:9).

He is waiting to forgive all your sins and to cleanse you from all unrighteousness. He has paid for all your sins on the Cross, but even after we become a child of God, we still commit acts of sin. In order to maintain a right relationship with our Heavenly Father, we must regularly seek His forgiveness when we disobey Him. God's forgiveness is a promise to remember our sin no more. When we confess our sin to Him, we are agreeing with God about our sin, which includes turning from that sin and a commitment to change. That confession restores the openness of our relationship with our heavenly Father. Though God has forgiven all our sins, the Christian walk is a process of bringing our lives more and more into line with God's standards.

My friend, take some time right now to be alone with God. Read Psalm 32:1-7 to see how David expressed the relief he felt after confessing his sins of adultery, murder and deception. Think back over your life and name the sins that still plague you with guilt.

Sins that still plague me:

Pray and ask God to forgive each of the sins you have named. When you come before God with a sincere heart asking Him to reveal ways you have sinned against Him, He will bring to mind areas that need to be confessed. Remember, my dear friend, He already knows everything about your life and yet He has loved you with an everlasting love (Jeremiah 31:3). He knows you and He is ready to forgive. The Bible assures us that nothing is too difficult for God (Jeremiah 32:17).

Day 17

Let's go back to the story of Joseph. He maintained a close relationship with God, refusing to sin against God with Potiphar's wife. He would have had to continually confess any known sin so that he could remain in fellowship with God in all of his circumstances. His traumatic transition to Egypt included many hurtful encounters with people. In order to remain useful, he could not allow bitterness to cloud his relationship with the Lord. So in each situation he had to forgive those who hurt him. Name the people from his father's house to Egypt that Joseph had to forgive to remain useful to God (Jeremiah 32:17).

How did this prepare Joseph for the reunion with his brothers?

List any people God has brought to your mind that you need to forgive.

You, too, can expect God's blessing as you obediently respond to the things you are learning from God's Word. While it may seem that you are in a dark place in your life, I pray that you too will trust Him for the dawning of a new day. This day can be very near. Once you repent and receive God's forgiveness for your sin, the fruit of that repentance will be seen in a desire to make all your other relationships right before God. In obedience to God, we are to forgive others as we have been forgiven and to love others as God has loved us. See what God has to say in Colossians 3:12-14.

Just as we are reconciled to God through repentance, our reconciliation is so important to God that He tells us to reconcile with our brother before we come to worship Him (Matthew 5:24). Let's go back to Genesis to see how God restored Joseph's relationships with his brothers. How old was Joseph when his brothers sold him into slavery? (Genesis 37:2).

Joseph would have been 39 years old when he saw his brothers again. How many years have passed?

Lets see how Joseph's reunion with his brothers worked out? Note Joseph's emotions.

1. What was Joseph's position? (Genesis 42:6).

2. Why do you think Joseph disguised himself and spoke harshly? (42:7). What was he trying to find out? Who was missing?

3. In Chapter 42:16 what was his test meant to reveal?

Joseph's brothers had deceived their father, Jacob, in the past and were living a lie. Truth is the basis of trust in any relationship. So when the truth has been compromised, it must be restored to reconcile the relationship. What relationships of yours may be affected by deception about your abortion?

Have you kept it a secret from your husband/family? Are you still living a lie?

Are you willing to endure the pain of exposure to be right before God and be at peace in your relationships as far as it depends on you? (Romans 12:18).

4. What did Joseph's test cause his brothers to recall in Genesis 42:18-22?

5. What was it that touched Joseph's emotions in verse 42:24?

6. Joseph must have mulled over many questions in his mind in the years since that caravan carried him away from his family and into Egypt. How he must have hurt to be rejected and sold by his own brothers. However, in Genesis 42:25-35 Joseph was gracious to his brothers. What do Matthew 18:21-22 and Romans 12:19-21 indicate had to happen in Joseph's heart for him to have this attitude?

7. When the brothers returned with Benjamin, Joseph was overcome with emotion again. Who was Joseph and Benjamin's mother? (Genesis 30:22-24; 35:16-19)_____ .

What happened to her?

Why do you think Joseph and Benjamin were special to Jacob?

How do you think the other brothers felt?

Why do you think Joseph had a hard time controlling his emotions when he saw Benjamin?

8. Read Genesis 45:1-15 and ask God to help you understand where Joseph was in his life. What do you think was going on in Joseph's mind and why did he weep so loudly?

9. Who did Joseph believe was responsible for his coming to Egypt? How did this enable Joseph to forgive his brothers? See Genesis 45:5-8.

10. What did Joseph's reconciliation with his brothers look like? What do you think their tears indicated?

The tears of emotion are associated with how we think about the things that have happened to us. Tears can mean many things, and although they do provide some relief, they may or may not be helpful in the long run. Tears may be over painful losses, unresolved conflicts, wrong choices, painful memories; or they may be tears of joy. Because tears often accompany abortion memories, it is important to biblically evaluate the cause of the tears in order to shed the light of God's Word on the thoughts that produce them. Have you lost hope over your painful loss? Are there strained or broken relationships? Is there something you want that you cannot get? Is there guilt over sin that has not been confessed? Are you hiding something that should be exposed? Or are yours tears of joy because God has set you free from your guilt and shame? Tears of true repentance bring cleansing and newness of life. See 2 Corinthians 7:10.

13. What do the following verses say about your relationship to others?

Matthew 5:24

Ephesians 4:32

Matthew 18:33-35

Colossians 3:13

Romans 12:17-18

Why is it important that you be reconciled with those you have hurt and those who have hurt you?

Who must you recognize as in charge of all that happens in your life for you to respond as Joseph? What promises can you claim by faith? (Hebrews 10:23; Romans 8:28-29).

When we trust God's promises in adverse circumstances, we demonstrate faith in God who has promised and cannot lie. Remember, my friend, there is nothing too difficult for God.

14. List the people with whom you have a broken relationship. Look back at your list of people to forgive. Are there other broken relationships you need to add to this list?

Ask God and another Godly person to help you know the right time and whether it is appropriate to seek reconciliation. Please remember, they may not all receive what you are saying with joy and compassion, but you are obeying God to seek forgiveness and reconciliation. Like Joseph, you must do what is right and trust God to work all things together for your good. He wants to make you more like Christ through the trials He allows to come your way.

In Matthew 6:12 Jesus said we are to forgive others as we have been forgiven. When God forgives us, it is because we humbly acknowledge our sin and desire to turn away from it (Luke 18:13-14). We are indebted to God and He chooses to forgive us because the Lord Jesus paid the debt we owe God. When He forgives us He promises to no longer hold that debt against us. So when you forgive someone you are essentially making a promise to no longer hold that offense against them. That will mean you can't talk about the offense to others in the wrong way or dwell on it any longer yourself. When the offense is no longer separating you, you are free to rebuild your relationship based on truth and love.

Day 18

As we go back to the story of Joseph, although he had forgiven his brothers, there was still unfinished business.

Read Genesis 50:15-21 again.
1. What event caused Joseph's brothers to bring up the past again? What did they fear? (vs. 15).

2. What does their question reveal about their guilt? (vs. 16-18).

3. How did their specific request help to clear the air? (vs. 19-21). List the ways Joseph revealed his genuine heart of forgiveness in Genesis 50:19-21.

4. What must you do to prepare your heart for this kind of genuine forgiveness? Are you ready to forgive those who have hurt you? Have you received God's forgiveness and do you recognize what it cost God to forgive you? Have you acknowledged God's purposes are good and are you willing to trust His plan for you?

What should your heart look like? (Psalm 51:10).

What other command does forgiveness fulfill?
(1 Corinthians 13:4-5; Ephesians 5:2).

How do you prepare your heart to forgive another?
(Philippians 2:3-4; Colossians 3:12-14).

How can you prepare your heart to seek forgiveness?
(Psalm 51:17; I John 1:9).

How are wrongs that we cannot make right resolved?
(Romans 12:17-19).

What heart attitude must you maintain to be right before God?
(Luke 6:35-37).

5. Go back to your list of those you have hurt and/or those who have hurt you. If there has been a continual struggle in your mind and the other person knows there is a strain between you, you should go to that person to be reconciled with them. (Caution: If either you or your partner in conceiving your aborted child is now married to another, it is best not to pursue reconciliation with him. Be sure you have forgiven him in your heart so that you are ready to make it right if the opportunity ever presents itself.) Using a separate sheet of paper for each person, write out what you should say to each one. Be sure to accept full responsibility for your sin without blaming anyone else. Go over your words with a trusted godly counselor or friend or if you are doing this study in a group maybe you can go over these with them. Pray for strength and wisdom from God. Plan how and when you will go to each person. Maybe you would like to make some notes below:

Do you realize that once you have reconciled your relationship with God and others, you can lead a peaceful normal life? Well, my friend, I can tell you it truly is possible. In the following lesson, I have written how God reconciled me with my daddy after deceiving him for many years. In restoring that relationship, God has shown me more of Himself as well. I trust that you will find hope in reading what only God could have done. Abundant blessings beyond my imagination have come through my Savior, Jesus Christ.

Day 19

My Story
Sandy Day

On November 19, 1992, God used a godly woman to help me begin to let go of my bitterness and resentment towards people surrounding my abortion. Before going through my long and exhausting list, I acknowledged my sin of abortion, and I knew then, that God had forgiven me because God keeps His promises. Exodus 34:6b-7a describes God as **"The Lord, the Lord God, compassionate and gracious, slow to anger, and abounding in lovingkindness and truth; who keeps lovingkindness for thousands, who forgives iniquity, transgression and sin."** That day, as I acknowledged and confessed my sin to God, I knew on the authority of His Word that God had forgiven me. It is the truth found in God's Word that sets us free (John 8:32). I could sum up that day with the Lord with this verse in Psalm 32:5:

> **"I acknowledged my sin to Thee, and my iniquity I did not hide; I said, I will confess my transgressions to the Lord; and Thou didst forgive the guilt of my sin."**

My guilt and shame were gone. Had I confessed my sin other times? Oh, yes! But those previous times I kept focusing on how badly I hurt rather than on God's merciful character, His promise of forgiveness, and His promise to no longer condemn me. Let's take some time right now to focus on the wonderful character of God. Name one of His characteristics from each of these passages.

Romans 8:1

Job 37:16

Psalm 139:1-6

Psalm 116:5

Lamentations 3:21-25

Nehemiah 9:31

Isaiah 55:8-9

1 John 1:8-9

John 4:16-19

Just remember, my friend, once you confess your sins, your true repentance will be evident with appropriate changes. Repentance and reconciliation are a work of God in your heart. Sincerity of heart is seen in a desire to please God by obeying His commands in Scripture. The psalmist's prayer after confession was **"Create in me a clean heart, O God, and renew a steadfast spirit within me" (Psalm 51:10).** God is pleased by the one whose heart is consistently His.

The Christmas after I dealt with my abortion, my husband, Craig, gave me a beautiful wrap band to go around my diamond. It was a reminder of the work God had done in my life to remove the guilt that had cast its shadow over our marriage and family for so long. The change in my life was that noticeable.

That was a special day when I realized I could start over. I had a new beginning -one in freedom, peace, and love. People at church even took time to tell me that I looked different. In the months that followed we saw Caleb Ministries (See Appendix III) grow by leaps and bounds. I knew that in His time, God would allow me to comfort others with the new comfort He had given me.

During the following summer, within a three-week time period, nine women called the ministry after having a stillborn child. I was still in amazement that God could use the precious life of our own stillborn son, Caleb, to help others who were hurting. Each woman who called about her stillbirth also previously had an abortion. I could hear in their voices that it was not easy to share this information. The timing of their calls on the heels of confessing my own abortion was very overwhelming to me. God used these conversations and my husband's encouragement to help me see that God wanted to use this part of my life to help others by showing them God's mercy and grace. My first response was "Oh, no! No way!" I was enjoying my new freedom from guilt, but to speak openly about my abortion was still unthinkable. Over a period of eight months God encouraged me through His Word and fellow believers to be open about my abortion so He could use it to bring comfort to other women who were still struggling. (1 Corinthians 2:3-4) Out of extreme gratitude for the overwhelming love and peace of God, I was compelled to tell others.

My husband and I began to pray and seek God's will concerning the next steps we should take. It seemed only right that if we were going to share this part of my story, we should begin by telling our pastor and Sunday school teacher. This was extremely hard because abortion was difficult to admit to ANYONE! Looking back to that day in the Pastor's office, I must have looked like a real mess as I started to cry uncontrollably. The Pastor ran to get lots of tissue from his restroom. My heart was hurting so badly, but I was determined to stop living a lie. God used their kind and understanding response to encourage me in speaking about my abortion to others. I will never forget the genuine love of God they showed me that day.

Their love and affirmation also led me to seek their prayer support as I went to face my daddy and confess my years of deception to him. I could not even fathom facing him, but I knew God wanted me to make it right with my family. My abortion was "the secret" that plagued our family for many years. I prayed for God's timing and trusted that He would give me the words to speak.

While I prayed for God's timing, I met with my sister and my mom to tell them I was going to reveal "the secret" to Daddy. They both said, "Are you sure?" I said, "Definitely, yes." This "secret" was a lie that my mom, my sister, and I had kept from my dad for 17 years. I was confident that if I obeyed God He would bless my obedience. I was ready to obey the One who had forgiven me so freely, but I had to keep my eyes on Him knowing that He was in control!

One Sunday night in church God confirmed in my heart that I should not delay going to my dad any longer. The next evening my parents and I had dinner together and talked about things in general. After dinner my dad asked what it was I had on my mind. I told him I needed to talk mainly with him because Mom already knew about it. Then I began to cry. I do not think my heart has ever hurt so badly. I conveyed to my dad that I had had an abortion at age 19 and that I knew that what I had done was sin and very wrong. I asked for his forgiveness for disobeying him and keeping it from him all these years. He assured me that he had committed sin as well and would not hold my sin against me. He was just very sorry that I had held it in for so long. He hugged me and said, "I love you very much." When I left their home that night, I knew I had obeyed God in confessing my sin and seeking forgiveness. From that day forward, what I had done was in God's Hands to use for His purposes.

Next, I arranged a meeting with our entire ministry staff at my house. I told them it was very important that each person be present. Everyone sat down and I told them about my "secret sin" and about my painful struggle in keeping it secret for so many years. I never wanted a soul to know. Everyone began to cry. Admitting my abortion to women who could not conceive and who had lost babies was nearly as hard as telling my parents. Later that evening, one girl confessed that she too had committed the sin of abortion and in the following weeks, several others in our ministry confessed to having an abortion. Each woman expressed gratitude for my willingness to acknowledge my sin and for my assurance of God's forgiveness. Seeing that it helped them come to terms with their own silent pain of abortion was very encouraging.

Energized by God's grace in forgiving me and setting me free, I met with some other close friends to tell them of God's mercy in forgiving my abortion. Even though the telling was still painful at times, God continually showed me that He wanted to use this story of His forgiveness to help others. Opportunities to share my testimony of His grace at work in me came from various ministries to women. Every time I spoke about my abortion and God's forgiveness, women would come to tell me they had been in my shoes or how our lives were similar. In hearing their stories, my heart broke for them. I was able to reassure each one that God is a forgiving God and that He can use even an abortion to bring good into our lives for His glory. I pray that each woman has found the peace of God that surpasses all understanding (Philippians 4:6-7).

As God continued to work in my heart after that heart-wrenching night in my parent's home, I wanted to write a letter to my daddy. At different times after our initial talk, I would refer to that time and my Dad would reassure me that he forgave me and that he hurt with me. This is the letter God laid on my heart as a benediction for all that has happened to our family. I pray it will be of comfort and encouragement to you.

Dear Precious Daddy,

Several instances have happened in the last few weeks that brought the reality of death to the forefront of my mind. I was overjoyed when you were told that the spot on your lung was a calcium deposit. While you were going through the tests I thought of words that I would want to say to you if something were seriously wrong. I decided to write them down and send them anyway because we never know the minute or the hour when it will be our last.

Even though I cannot erase the difficulties we had as a family, I have replaced those times with the many special memories I will cherish forever. All those times you rode the waves with me at the beach, all the times you took me to the park and played ball with me and all the swimming lessons were fun times for me. You let me wear your t-shirts after David died and Mom slept with me. The care you gave me was so special.

Daddy, the main reason I am writing this letter is to prepare you for a very special reunion you will have in heaven with three very special babies. The youngest in heaven would be four years old. I miscarried him during the time of the '92 election when Corey, Mama and I were in Lowell and President Bush was campaigning. A year later, after minor surgery, the Doctor informed Craig and me that it would be a miracle if we conceived again. God showed me to cherish everyday with Corey. I am so thankful the two of you have such a special relationship.

Our middle son, Caleb, has probably changed more lives in his short life than anyone I know. He would be 8 years old. Daddy, Caleb was so beautiful and I miss him so much. As a result of his short life many souls have been saved, a ministry was born, and my marriage was forever strengthened because of our tiny 3 lb 9 oz son. I am sure he radiates heaven.

My oldest child (I think of her as Abbey in my heart), would have been 17 years old now. She is the one I will desire to see the most because of all the grief and turmoil of my disobedience to terminate her precious life. I'm forever sorry I took the privilege away from you of being her Paw-Paw. Daddy, hold her extra long for me and tell her I will be there soon.

Daddy, I can't wait until that special day when I see you holding all my babies. What a grand reunion that will be! But Daddy I can't say that will be the first thing I want to see because there has been a Man who has comforted my weeping spirit in the wee hours of the night and wiped every tear from my face. He has replaced my sorrow with joy and turned my mourning into dancing. When I wasn't able, He was. When I was weak, He made me strong. Daddy, if it weren't for Him, the Lord Jesus, we wouldn't have the special relationship we have today. He makes all things beautiful in His time. After my glorious reunion with Him I'm sure as I look across that shore I'll probably see all my babies cuddled around their Paw-Paw each one wanting to be the closest to you.

Daddy, in closing, I have no regrets about anything. I would not have picked any other family to be a part of because God put me in the family He wanted me to be in. But Daddy, above all else, I would choose you to be my Daddy because you are the most special daddy in the whole world.

I love you with all my heart,
Your baby,
Sandy

107

Before openly confessing my abortion, I would not have believed that God had plans for me to reveal my sin of abortion. I cannot even begin to count how many women have written me, called, or spoken to me about their own personal and silent pain. I am overwhelmed at how God has used the very thing I wanted to conceal forever to bring blessing to my life and to others. Has it been painful at times? Yes. It was not easy going back to the pastor, our Sunday school teacher, Daddy, family, and then ministry associates and friends. Any pain, however, is far outweighed in seeing God reconcile my family and mend our broken relationships. Our loving heavenly Father delights in showing mercy. God met me at the Cross with His forgiveness. In return, I have been blessed with peace, comfort, and the joy of helping others find mercy in the midst of their pain.

My friend, He wants to heal your broken heart and bring comfort to your spirit. As you have read the verses and pondered the questions, you may have some questions of your own. Do not put off making things right any longer. If you would like more help, seek the counsel of your pastor or a godly Christian friend.

Chapter 5

"And we know that God causes all things to
work together for good to those who love God,
to those who are called according to His purpose."
Romans 8:28

Hope for the Future

Stories of Hope

Day 20

A Love That Would Not Let Me Go
Kimberly Lorenzini

In the waiting room of the doctor's office, I sat, my head propped in my hands - daydreaming. I was only vaguely aware of the sound of a baby crying. Glancing over, I saw the little one, sitting with her visibly pregnant mom. I was happy to retreat to my own world. Looking out the window I imagined the touch of the mid-summer sunshine falling across my face, the smell of fresh green grass mixed with wild flowers - and him. In my dream my handsome husband takes my hand and walks our son and me to the playground. This man makes me feel safe and secure. I know he will never hurt me or leave me. Ours would be a "happily ever after" story.

Reality snatched away the moment. And I wondered if it would steal away the dream altogether. From the window I saw Chad, sitting on his car smoking a cigarette. "Just have the abortion," I told myself. "We are too young to be parents."

When I met Chad I had no intention of starting a serious relationship. I was just a high school freshman after all. Chad was a year older and very handsome. I couldn't believe he would even want to talk to me. He was perfect in every way. I loved that he paid attention to me and thought I was beautiful. Every night, he called me to say goodnight.

Our four years together had not been easy. Friends told me they saw him with other girls. My heart was broken again and again as I wrestled with the question, "Why am I not enough for him? What am I missing?" I didn't have the courage to do what I needed to do - I realize now I missed out on school and girl friends. But, at the time, I thought he was all I wanted - even if he hurt me. A reassuring word and a glance from those electric blue eyes was all it took to convince me that I was being too jealous, that he was committed to me, and that we would always be together.

We actually broke up for two months after Chad went to college, while I was in my last year of high school. But his charm won me over again. This time I was walking down the stage to be crowned Homecoming Princess. He had some of his fraternity brothers hold up a big sign that said he loved me and needed me in his life. Everyone at school thought that was true love. I was overwhelmed. True love was something I longed to have.

Two weeks after that night, I went in the doctor's office, pregnant and facing the hardest decision of my life. I was there for an abortion. Chad had been willing to support whatever choice I made. He said, "We don't have to do this. We could get in my car and drive away. We could get married and start a family." But I had earned a college scholarship. I had a bright future ahead of me. Besides, I couldn't bear the thought of telling my parents. Fear drove me to a decision I would soon regret.

I remember wondering how things might have been different if leukemia hadn't taken my real dad's life when I was five. My family and I thought we had done all the "right things" to make sure God spared his life. We prayed. We lighted candles for him daily. Still he slipped away, and I gave up on the idea of a loving God. Six years later I had a new dad - a police officer who brought four children of his own to our blended family. My hopes for regaining a sense of love and security ran high. But a year later, my stepfather, the one I hoped would provide love and security for me, began to sexually abuse me.

The waiting room had been crowded. Every chair was filled and others stood. "We couldn't all be making a mistake, could we?" I wondered. After a 3-hour wait, I was growing anxious. Chad came in to sit, then left to smoke again. I just wanted it to be over.

Finally, the receptionist called my name and led me to a counseling room. There, a middle-aged woman told me to watch a video, inserted the tape and walked out. I felt so alone. Some of the girls on the screen chose adoption. But I felt I could never carry a child just to give her away. What if she were to come and find me someday to tell me what a bad mother I had been? Besides there was that other secret nobody knew about.

Bulimia. I called it "just keeping my weight down." My mother had always warned me of the importance of first impressions. Girls who were going to be "somebody," weren't chubby. I had been purging my body since I was 14. Lots of times my abused body felt the effects. No, abortion was the only option I felt I could consider.

"Sign these papers," the woman said upon reentering the room. "Now," she continued very routinely, "what are some reasons you want this procedure done today?" I took a deep breath and repeated the words that I had forced myself to say all day long: "I just received a scholarship to college. I am going to be somebody. I cannot have a baby." The woman smiled and assured me I was making a good decision and that everything would be okay. I took some comfort in her words.

In another room, an ultrasound was performed. The attending nurse continued to walk in and out of the room. I wondered if something was wrong. I heard her say, "I can't find anything. We might have an ectopic pregnancy." My counselor informed me that an ectopic pregnancy meant that it had to be removed or would cause death. Immediately the lady came back into the room, accompanied by a tall man in a white coat. I tried to stay focused on the questions my counselor was asking me: "What profession do you want to go into?" "Where are your friends going to college?" They continued to move the probe over me and look at the screen. My counselor held my hand.

Then came the sound of a vacuum. I looked at my counselor and blurted out, "Did I tell you I just got a scholarship to college and was nominated for Who's Who of American High School Students?" I whispered to myself, "I'm going to be somebody."

In the recovery room I was given juice and crackers and told to stay there until I felt ready to walk. The woman next to me told me this was her third abortion. I could not stay there any longer. I left even though I still felt dizzy.

"What to Expect Now" read the heading on the paper the nurse gave me as I left. For the first time, I read that potential problems associated with my abortion, included heavy bleeding, possible hemorrhaging, future miscarriage, and impaired future fertility. The list continued but the tears that welled up kept me from finishing. I was advised that I would probably have cramps "no stronger than my period." If they worsened, I was to contact my doctor.

The nausea started later that evening. Cramps followed. They were not so bad at first, but by the end of dinner they were getting worse. My family and I were finishing our decorating for Christmas, now just two weeks off. Even as I smiled and helped decorate the tree, I wondered if anyone would catch me wincing in pain, or notice a look of guilt, of sadness or shame that I felt taking over my mind and my heart.

Two months later, Chad and I were still together but he began to tell me that I wasn't any fun anymore - that I had changed. My guess is that I just wasn't the same with him. I felt numb and I wasn't up to pretending that I was still a happy-go-lucky kid. My innocence was gone. My trust in Chad was gone. Even when we continued having sex, there was dullness, a heaviness that wouldn't go away. I didn't even really want to have sex with him anymore, but he kept begging and I always gave in. I began to hate him for that and to hate myself for betraying myself.

That summer I resolved to change my life and to forget my past. I started dating other guys. On occasion, Chad and I went out. When we did, I felt the pain of it all sweep over me again.

A year after the abortion, I was in college, working to prove that my choice was not in vain - that I would succeed in life. I moved into an apartment with two friends, where I learned to escape in the party life. There I could forget the past. There I didn't have to think.

But parties inevitably end. And in every place, in every decision, my life was affected by my abortion decision. After my classes, I worked at a preschool center. Inside I was secretly hoping that I could make up for what I had done. But there was pain there too. I would look at those kids and wonder, what would my child have looked like? There were even times when I was afraid to touch or carry them. What if I hurt them? Do I really deserve to care for children when I couldn't even take responsibility for my own? I felt I deserved the punishment of not enjoying children.

Then came the night my friend Samantha died. We had planned to meet at 9:30 pm at the McDonald's ® across town. I arrived a half hour late, so she left without me. Witnesses said she ended up at a party and went for a ride with a guy in his new car. She loved cars. The accident report said both of them were legally drunk. "If I had been there on time, would things be different?" I couldn't help but wonder. "Could I have prevented it? Would I have died with her?"

114

Samantha had grown up in a Christian home, but had never mentioned her faith. It seemed the whole town turned out for her funeral. The pastor talked a lot about Heaven. He talked about Christ dying on the cross for our sins.

I looked at her in the casket one last time, a final glimpse of her to remember forever. As I did, I turned and studied her mother for a moment. She was crying, and her husband's arms held her, keeping her from collapsing. "Is that how a mom is to mourn for her child?" I questioned. "Should we weep and let the whole world know we no longer have our baby?"

I felt a deep sense of grief for my friend, Samantha. Further, her death forced me to think about my own father - and about my baby. Is my baby in Heaven? I felt very alone in dealing with my abortion. Abortion is a subject that is easy to talk about before it becomes personal. There had been a time when I was convinced that abortion is simply a woman's right. But once abortion became part of my own experience I discovered its secret shame.

Two months after that funeral, we threw a big party for my roommate's 21st birthday. Some of Samantha's other friends joined us. It felt good to be together, like we all shared the same heartache. Brent was one of her friends. He invited us to a Bible study his mom was starting. I laughed out loud. He continued, saying it would be interesting to try to understand what happened to Samantha after death. Even through the blare of the music, the laughing, the noise of the crowd, I heard that invitation and I was intrigued by it.

Bible study wasn't at all what I expected. We all sat around together, Bibles in our laps, looking up Scripture and talking about how it applied to our lives. I listened, but without believing. I kept wondering just what these Christians wanted from me. Do they just want to be able to say they had a good "turn out" ? Were they going to ask me for money?

In those first weeks, I learned that the Bible says that God is my provider (Genesis 22:1-14), and that He is trustworthy - even when I do not see how, circumstances can work out for good in the end. I heard that God is the Lord who heals (Exodus 15:22-26), and that He is like a parent to me; directing me and keeping me safe. These were radical statements.

I hid my internal struggle behind intellectual questions. At the Bible study I openly argued, "How can you know that Christianity is the true religion? How can you say we have to believe in Jesus to go to Heaven?" Yet, on the inside I felt convicted. I knew I was a sinner. I wondered what it meant to "give my life to Christ." Would I have to leave everything and everyone I know? Again, fear kept me moving, only this time toward God.

"I'm not coming back," I told Lorie, the Bible study leader. But the issues God had allowed to surface continued to haunt me. "If there is a God, then why did He let so much happen to me? Why didn't He heal my Dad? Why didn't He stop my stepfather?" I knew Lorie was stating the truth when she said to me, "Kim, you seem to need all the answers before you trust that Christ is who He says He is. But when you die and stand before Him you will have no excuse. You heard His message and are refusing it."

My disease of the spirit - my unbelief - plagued me in much the same way that bulimia continued to steal life from my physical body. At 22, I had continued my destructive cycle for eight years. I called Overeaters Anonymous once, but then I didn't have the courage to stay on the line. God was aware of my desperate need - both physically and spiritually.

One night I was feeling particularly alone. Despair pulled at me. My response was to order a large pizza and polish off the whole thing. "I have to get it out!" I screamed to myself. So, I did my usual trip to the bathroom and threw it up. Suddenly I felt light-headed and that nagging pain in my chest. I promised myself this would be the last time. Then everything went dark and I felt myself slip to the floor. There's no one to save me, I thought in my helplessness. "What if I die? Where will I go? How can Jesus forgive me?"

The truths shared at the Bible study returned to me at that frightening moment. The words I had heard with my ears, began to make sense: Believe that Jesus is God and can take away sin. I still didn't understand it all, but - at that moment - I did believe. "You are God," I declared to myself and to God. "I believe you can forgive me. Please forgive me. But can you forgive murder? I killed my baby. It was sin. I always knew it was wrong."

I lay on the floor for a long time. I continued to ask God to forgive me. I realized that there was no other hope for me - no other way out of the mess I had made. I prayed and cried there, on the cold hard floor, until I finally slept.

When I returned to Bible study the following week, I listened with new understanding. If there were answers for me in the Bible, I was committed to finding them - and believing them. My lonely meeting with God had convinced me that God knew everything about me (John 3:19-20) and loved me anyway!

My first lesson as a new believer was about the seriousness of sin and its destructive nature. That meant dealing with my abortion. God showed me the selfishness that was at the root of my decision to abort. He knew I had hoped to escape the responsibility for my sinful choice to have sex outside of marriage (Hebrews 13:4). He also knew that I took the life of my child because I didn't want to be burdened with a baby.

As I looked back on that dark time following the abortion, it struck me that so many of my decisions then were based on my need to push the reality of a baby out of my mind. I had built a wall of denial in order to protect myself from the pain of guilt in admitting that I took the life of my own child. But all my efforts to forget didn't take away the guilt and shame I felt before God.

My next step had to be admitting that my sin - all the ways I had violated God's commands in my life - kept me from a relationship with a holy God. When I came to understand that Jesus was the only One who could take that sin from me and could reconcile me to the Father, then - and only then - could I stop trying to heal myself, stop trying to make up for my past. In God's Word, I learned that God promises to heal me from my pain of guilt and to carry my sorrow. He has taken the punishment I deserve as a sinner, and delivered me from an eternity apart from Him. Jesus made it all possible by dying on the Cross, then rising again to show Himself to be stronger than death. A tremendous burden was lifted from me.

Four years into my journey with Christ, I participated in a Post Abortion Counseling and Education class. It was during that very special learning and sharing time that God led me to understand what He alone had done for me on the cross, and I asked Him to forgive me for my abortion. In the Old Testament book of Micah, the prophet declares that God pardons iniquity. He does not keep His anger. He will have compassion on us, "casting our sin into the depths of the sea." This was what I had truly longed for all my life - God's forgiveness. Love from my parents, boyfriend, or friend was never enough. What I desired, above all else, was to know that God would forgive me for everything and still love me.

Like so many post-abortive women, however, shame continued to be an obstacle for me. I feared rejection from those who might learn of my past. To protect myself, I shared my secret with very few. Again, God used the Bible Study class to instruct me on just that issue. In Isaiah 54:4, God states, **"Do not fear, for you will not be ashamed; neither be disgraced, for you will not be put to shame; for you will forget the shame of your youth, And will not remember the reproach of your widowhood anymore." (NKJV)** In verses 7 and 8, the passage reads, **"For a mere moment I have forsaken you, but with great mercies I will gather you. With little wrath I hide my face from you for a moment; but with everlasting kindness I will have mercy on you, says the Lord your redeemer." (NKJV)** As I meditated on these words, God released me from the guilt and shame of my sin.

Memories of my abortion return now and then. I often have to remind myself that I am truly forgiven and deeply loved by God. These memories, however, are no longer characterized by pain, guilt or shame. With joy I anticipate seeing my child in Heaven. There will always be someone missing in my life. I may have to face infertility. The future may bring the sadness of knowing that my child missed the experience of a loving family. These are earthly consequences of my sin. But I have hope in knowing that there are no eternal consequences for my sin, because Jesus paid the price for me. I've been forgiven and set free. You can be, too.

What a wonderful God we have. He is the Father of our Lord Jesus Christ, the source of every mercy, and the One who so wonderfully comforts and strengthens us in our hardships and trials. And why does He do this? One reason is so that when others are troubled, needing our sympathy and encouragement, we can pass on to them this same help and comfort God has given us (2 Corinthians 1:3-4).

Kimberly's UPDATE:

Today, Kimberly is happily married to a godly man. Shortly after their marriage, they both attended and graduated with degrees from New Orleans Baptist Theological Seminary. Presently, Kimberly is serving at the Pregnancy Resource Center of the San Fernando Valley in CA. They believe that to truly help a client they need to share the truth of Christ and the new life He can offer her. God has been so good to Kimberly! They are hoping to start a family soon.

Personally to you...

1. How were you encouraged after reading Kimberly's story?

2. How did you identify with her story?

3. Below are a few Scripture passages Kimberly used. Which one(s) could you apply to your circumstance(s)? How do they help you?

    • John 3:19-20

- Isaiah 54:4

- II Corinthians 1:3-4

Day 21

The Forever Love I Found
Debby Mylar

In the first chapter of 1 Corinthians, Paul talks about how God delights to choose those whom the world regards as foolish, to shame the wise. The point: the seemingly wise of this world are, in reality, fools because they are blind and do not know God. I was once that "wise" person of the world. No longer. Now it is my privilege to declare that I am a fool in the eyes of this world, but wise in Christ. Not because of anything I have done, but because of Jesus who lives inside of me. He is wisdom in me.

My twin sister and I were the last of five girls born to my family. Although ours was a Jewish family, I never learned much about the Jewish faith. We never went to Temple. All I knew for sure was that Jews did not accept Christ as the Messiah. We did, however, celebrate the high holidays. I remember enjoying Hanukah, with its presents, but disliking Passover, with its solemnity. Religious people struck me as hypocritical. Worse still, being Jewish made me feel different - even unattractive, especially because I inherited the "traditional" Jewish nose.

Our house was a place of many rules and few expressions of love and encouragement. As a result, I drew my emotional support from my involvement in sports and from a married couple for whom I babysat. The wife was like a sister to me. I confided in her about my friends and about boys. Her husband helped me with my homework and even taught me how to drive a car.

I spent a lot of time in their home. The summer I turned 17, I spent a week at their house while my family was moving. Frequently, the wife would go to bed and the husband would stay up and talk with me. One night, after his wife had gone to bed, he molested me. I did not know what to do. I didn't think I could tell either his wife or my family. I considered talking about it with my twin sister, but I felt guilty somehow and decided not to tell anyone. I felt that my dream of purity before marriage had been shattered.

Confused and naive, I convinced myself that I was in love with this man. For a year, we carried on a sexual relationship. It wasn't until I entered college and grew interested in someone my own age that I finally saw how foolish it would be to marry a man twice my age. It was then that I started dating Steve, an engineering student who lived in the same dorm with me. I held off having sex with him until I felt confident that we would get married someday. We dated throughout our college years and all our friends were convinced that we would marry after college.

Meanwhile, the summer between my junior and senior years of college, I was involved in a study that involved running. The purpose of the study was to investigate why some women lose their menstrual cycle with intense exercise. For two months, all the study participants spent their days and nights together. Each woman worked up to running 10 miles per day for 5 days a week. I am very competitive in nature, as was one other woman in the study. After a few weeks, I discovered that this other woman was a lesbian. Though I thought this was strange, I liked her and enjoyed the fact that she paid a lot of attention to me. Eventually, there was a sexual encounter.

When I returned to school, I had every intention of picking up where Steve and I left off - on the road to matrimony. I even told him about the lesbian encounter. While he didn't seem overly concerned, it wasn't long before he told me that he was interested in dating other women. At the same time, he was preparing - mentally and emotionally - for his upcoming move to graduate school in California. It was clear to me that Steve was distancing himself from me.

During this final year of college, my father died after years of chronic illness. While I had never been close to my father, a very private man, this loss, together with the uncertainty of my relationship with Steve, left me wondering what I should do after college. In hopes of regaining ground with Steve, I decided to find a job in California to be near him. When the job came through, I was convinced things were finally back on track.

But there came another unexpected turn. The night before I left Boston to go to Santa Barbara, California to start my new job, I went to a party with Dennis, a classmate and friend. We both had too much to drink, and it became a night I will always regret. The next morning as I hurried to catch my flight, feeling bleary-eyed and betrayed, I remember a fear of pregnancy flashing through my mind.

It was quickly replaced by more immediate concerns: a place to live, transportation, and my new career in physical therapy.

Once in California, I found an apartment and some female roommates. Things were just starting to settle down when I realized I had missed a period. This had never happened to me, even in the course of the running study. My new gynecologist told me it was too early to worry, that I might be experiencing a delayed reaction. But a few more weeks bore out the truth: I was pregnant. My first action was to arrange for an abortion.

In my mind, I had no choice. I was just starting my career. I had no family or good friends living close to me. How could I possibly have a child under these circumstances? As the time drew near, I remembered a paper I had done in high school on abortion. My position: pro-choice. My parents read that paper and never disagreed with me. In fact, I never remember anyone disagreeing with me. I had never talked with anyone who thought abortion was wrong. And yet, at that moment, it felt wrong. One of my new roommates took me to my appointment.

I determined to handle the procedure in a very mechanical way. Refusing to let myself think emotionally about what I was doing, I concentrated only on what had to be done to keep my goals and career on course. I would not consider the possibility that I was killing a baby. It really was not until I was a Christian that I realized that I had murdered a human being. That child would have been 17 years old this year.

I quickly put the event behind me, mentioning it to no one. I did not miss one day of work and barely missed any days of running! I continued to date men, all the time growing more disillusioned that my love interests were more interested in sex than love. In my job, I worked with quite a few lesbians. I decided that I had had enough of men and that I could relate better with women. I pursued a lesbian lifestyle in earnest.

In Romans 1:24-26, Paul writes about God giving **"wicked men over in the sinful desires of their hearts to sexual impurity for the degrading of their bodies with one another. They exchanged the truth of God for a lie, and worshiped and served created things rather than the Creator... Because of this, God gave them over to shameful lusts. Even their women exchanged natural relations for unnatural ones.. (NIV)"** God clearly gave me over to my sinful desires. In the midst of living this lifestyle, I moved to Salt Lake City for graduate school and to chase a relationship with a woman I had met in California that lived in Salt Lake. When this relationship failed, I searched until I found someone else to love me.

At the age of 25, I found myself very successful in the world's eyes. I had a great career in management at a major medical center; I was an adjunct faculty member at a university; I was preparing to run my second marathon; and I had found a lover with whom I shared a house. No one knew that inside I was empty and I was very depressed. So, like everyone else I knew, I decided I needed therapy.

But it wasn't therapy that rescued me at this low point in my life. It was during this same time that my twin sister surrendered her life to Christ at college. While visiting her there, she introduced me to Frank, who eventually became my husband. Frank had a girlfriend at the time and was well aware of my lifestyle, but my sister thought we would hit it off as friends. Secretly, she hoped Frank might be able to reach me spiritually. We became immediate friends, often exchanging letters and phone calls. Strangely, I sensed in my heart that if God were real, I would find Him. Frank asked me to read the book, *More Than A Carpenter* by Josh McDowell. As I became acutely aware of my sin, I thought I could never be "good" enough to become a Christian. I did not realize that was the very point each of us has to reach, understanding that we can never be good enough to be accepted by God.

Since church was still out of the question for me, I started attending Bible studies at the Campus Christian Center. There, a pastor was teaching a series on the Tabernacle from the book of Leviticus. He impressed me with his knowledge of the Bible so I made an appointment to go and talk to him. The first thing he said to me was that he was envious that I was Jewish. That really took me by surprise since I was always embarrassed about being Jewish. He spent about two hours with me sharing various Scripture verses about how I could have a right relationship with God. I finally gave my heart to Christ. My search for true love had finally ended!

It seemed that immediately after surrendering my life to Christ, my eyes were opened to the truth of the Bible. I acknowledged my sin and received the forgiveness declared in Scripture: "Praise the LORD, O my soul, and forget not all his benefits; who forgives all your sins and heals all your diseases," (Psalm 103:3-4 - NIV). I rejoiced to discover that, "As far as the east is from the west, so far has He removed our transgressions from us" (Psalm 103:12 - NIV). I knew the blood of Jesus Christ had washed my sins away and I wanted nothing to do with my old ways. That meant I had to end my lesbian relationship and give up my entire lifestyle. God even made that easy. Within two weeks, I was living a brand new life - and I became engaged to Frank.

Frank and I succeeded in our commitment to wait until marriage to have sex. I did harbor fears that the scars from the sexual sin in my past would plague our marriage. This did not have to be true. Jesus Christ bore the penalty of my sin in His body when He died on Calvary, but I held on to those memories and resurrected them off and on after we were married. That was wrong. My past is completely forgiven and completely in the past (1 Corinthians 6: 9-11), indeed dead. That realization has brought so much freedom to me and to our marriage.

After three years of marriage, Frank and I became pregnant with our first child. I did not tell anyone I was pregnant for three months for fear of a miscarriage. But God graciously allowed Jessica to be born healthy. A few years later, we decided to have a second child. We got pregnant right away. I was still nervous for the health of the baby, but after three months it was Frank who faced a life-threatening illness. After being diagnosed with a high-risk testicular cancer, he underwent numerous surgeries. We were counseled to put away sperm if we thought we would want more children. No, our family was complete, we thought.

A few months after the birth of our son, we decided that we really would like to have at least one more child. A year or so later, I got pregnant again - something of a miracle considering Frank's cancer. This time I wasn't concerned at all, but 12 weeks into the pregnancy I experienced some bleeding. An ultrasound revealed that the baby had died and I would miscarry in the next few days. I felt as though the Lord had prepared me in my thoughts and, when it happened, I was surprised to find that I didn't despair. Instead, I was overwhelmed with the peace, joy, and presence of the Lord.

In another 6 months I was pregnant again. It seemed like such a long time to us. In retrospect, I believe God was preparing me throughout the pregnancy for what would come next. I never could see myself nursing the baby or taking care of him. I waited until three weeks before I was due to start taking out clothes and setting up the changing table. One week later, there was no heartbeat. I knew our son had died.

I chose to be induced right away. On the labor and delivery floor we were met by our pastor and some close friends who joined us in a time of weeping, praying and singing. It was sweet fellowship. Twelve hours later I delivered a beautiful little boy, perfect in every way except that his umbilical cord had been kicked off of the placenta, causing him to bleed to death. In the weeks that followed, God showed me that he had a purpose for Jake's life, even though he never got the chance to take a breath. We had an incredible funeral/dedication service for him. The Gospel was clearly presented to many who had never heard it. The Lord filled Frank and me with such joy, peace, and comfort that we were a mystery to all, even many Christians. God was most definitely glorified through the death of our son.

Our trust in God grew through this experience, even as He allowed us to struggle with the question of whether the loss had been God's "pay back" for my abortion. One night, Frank and I sat down and wrestled with this haunting accusation. But God clearly showed us that He does not work that way. The sin of abortion had been washed clean through the blood of Jesus Christ on the Cross. I realized I had to accept that God loves me and His purposes are always for good in my life, even if it doesn't appear that way at the time.

Three months later, I was pregnant again. I was awed to hear that the due date of this child was identical to Jake's. In my pride, I thought that God was rewarding us for how well we handled Jake's death. But after nine weeks, this baby also died. I meditated on God's Word during that time, **"For my thoughts are not your thoughts, neither are your ways my ways," declares the Lord. "As the heavens are higher than the earth, so are my ways higher than your ways and my thoughts than your thoughts" (Isaiah 55:8-9).** While this loss was probably the most difficult for me, I began to see God using it in my life. This was the time when I learned to cry out to the Lord, even as David did in the Psalms. I spent hours in that book of the Bible. David expressed my pain so much better than I could. In time I saw that my focus should not be on myself, but totally on the Lord and what He desires for me.

Like clockwork, three months found me pregnant again. As a family, we learned to trust God day by day, not knowing if Rachel would live or not. Again and again, the children asked if they were going to have a living, breathing sister. I couldn't promise. We just thanked God for every kick. My daughter prayed fervently that her sister would be part of the Mylar family on earth. Still, it was only when the nurses told me that I could push that I actually really let myself think that I might take this child home with me.

A year after Rachel was born I got pregnant again but miscarried after 10 weeks. While I still have a desire for another child, the Lord has taught me over the past few years to be content. I will be thankful for what the Lord has given us.

In looking back over my life, I see clearly my years of searching for love. The disappointments I have experienced since becoming a Christian have never detracted from the forever love I found when I met Jesus Christ. Knowing Him has brought peace to my restless soul. And He also has comforted me with the knowledge that there is no sin that Christ cannot forgive. Satan's greatest weapon against me has been the guilt of my past. I would choose to hide it, but God, in His wisdom, wants to use my past to reveal His power and His glory by demonstrating how He alone transformed my life.

Debby's Update:
The Lord has blessed Frank and Debby with four wonderful children whom she also has the privilege of home schooling. Frank is a Christian attorney, involved in partisan state politics in Utah. Today Debby co-leads a Homeschool Discipleship Support Group and serves on the Board for the Pregnancy Resource Center of Salt Lake City. Together, Frank and Debby are active in Bible Study Fellowship (BSF) and discipling couples.

Personally to you...
1. What encouraged you after reading Debby's story?

2. How did you identify with her story?

3. Below are a few Scripture passages Debby used. Which one(s) could you apply to your circumstance(s)? How do they help you?

    • Psalm 103:12

    • 1 Corinthians 6: 9-11

    • Isaiah 55:8-9

Day 22

God Uses Broken Vessels
Chris Nelson

The story I want to share with you is one of miraculous change. It is about how God brought me from the depths of sin and despair and gave me hope and joy. This is His story...this is what God has done for me.

Looking back now, it's not hard to understand how I came to make the bad choices I did. I never experienced family life as God meant it to be. My mom was married three times - twice divorced and once widowed. Each of the men she married was an alcoholic and was physically abusive to her, including my dad - husband number two. I was only three years old when my parents divorced. After that, the only time I really saw my dad was on my birthday or Christmas. It was not until after the loss of her third husband that my mother became a Christian.

The youngest of seven children, I grew up in a home where, understandably, my mother had little time for me. Most of her day was spent working to keep food on the table. I was left pretty much on my own. By age 12, I was dressing to get the attention I missed at home. I entered the adult world, becoming sexually active, by about my thirteenth birthday.

In October 1971 I married Mark. Shortly thereafter I felt the excitement and passion leave our marriage and fighting ensued. Less than a year into my marriage I discovered I was pregnant. I was 19 years old, married to someone I wasn't even sure I liked anymore, and pregnant with our first child. After the birth of our daughter, we moved to Connecticut near Mark's family. While my husband and I attended church together, neither of us had a relationship with the Lord.

As time went on, our marriage floundered. In a search for intimacy missing from our relationship, I became involved with a married man. In time, I became pregnant again, and was overcome with fear. I knew what I had been doing was wrong - that adultery was contrary to God's will, and I also knew I was not carrying my husband's baby. I was certain that my pregnancy was God's punishment for my sin. My perception of God was that He was all about judgment and punishment. I didn't know of His love and forgiveness.

With fear and panic overtaking me, I confided in two people. They both advised abortion. I followed their advice within two days by making an appointment for the abortion. When I told Mark I was pregnant, I let him believe the baby was his for fear he would leave me if he knew the truth. Using finances and my new job as excuses, I talked him into letting me abort the child. In truth I gave him little choice. In my heart, I knew that my marriage to Mark was weak, but I was unwilling to end it. So I took matters into my own hands.

I went for the abortion. Everything seemed so casual. There were other women there and all of them appeared to be handling the situation just fine. I spoke to one woman who was also married. Her remarks that she just didn't want another child made me feel better for the moment, as I echoed her words. Abortion seemed to be the only reasonable solution. Then I met with the counselor - or so-called counselor. Her only question to me was about what I wanted. That was the extent of my counseling: no facts, no explanation of the procedure or the risks, no mention of fetal development. "Is this what you want to do?" came the question. Of course, that is what I thought I wanted to do at the time.

All proceeded smoothly up to the point when I was put to sleep. I remember just as I was going out, a tear rolled down my face. "Why am I crying?" I wondered to myself. Oh, if only I had realized that day that I was taking a precious innocent life that God created and gave to me. If only someone had shown me a fetal model and let me see how my baby was being knit together by God. If only I had trusted Him enough to face the truth, whatever the outcome. If only I had known at the time how I would be haunted by the painful question, "Why did I do it?"

When I woke up the day after the abortion, I felt empty and sad. Yes, the panic was gone and I felt like everything had been resolved. No one would ever know my terrible sin. For five years I was in denial about the abortion. I continued my life, my routine, just as if nothing had ever happened. Mark and I never talked about it, just as we never talked about anything. I struggled to put my life in order, to be good and live up to what I thought God expected of me. But I knew I kept coming up short.

Mark and I were attending church but I always left feeling empty because God's Word was not being taught. I guess, deep down, I felt as if I could never be close to God because I was too wicked. When we heard about a church where the minister was really on fire for God, Mark and I decided to visit. On our first visit, the Pastor preached on abortion. The message was powerful and to the point. I'll never forget the shame I felt as He spoke. It was as if I wore a big red A on my back. Was everyone looking at me? I couldn't wait to get out of there. At home, I cried and cried, promising myself I would never go back to that place. But I did. The preaching I heard there convicted my heart of sin and awakened my desire for Jesus. I felt lonely for Him, and wanted, more than anything, to be clean and whole, and to feel His presence in my life.

After a year of attending that church body, I confessed my sin and asked Christ to take control of my life. He became my Savior. It was glorious to know that God loved and accepted me after all I had done. It was 1982 and shortly thereafter, we found out we were going to move to Charlotte, NC. As we prepared for the move, our pastor told us of a Bible-believing church we should check out. We had no idea what God had in store for us there.

As we stepped into this Charlotte church, I immediately felt the presence of God. God's Word was powerfully preached. And, as God would have it, it seemed that every sermon mentioned abortion. Each time it was mentioned, I felt as if a knife was going through my heart. I would go home feeling worthless and would beat myself up over how foolish I had been. A particularly painful moment came when Mark and I viewed a film discussing abortion and all that a baby endures in the course of the procedure. Again, I found myself weeping. My grief became deep and out of control.

This wasn't what I had anticipated from our move at all. In fact, when I left Connecticut, I believed I was leaving my garbage behind. I thought I could make a fresh start. No one would ever have to know about the old me. That worked for a while, but soon it was evident that I had packed my pain together with my other belongings and it remained with me. But God had a plan. He wanted me to bring it all with me so I could turn it all over to Him, once and for all, and find total forgiveness and cleansing.

Our new church just happened to be the same one attended by the director of the city's Crisis Pregnancy Center. And it also happened that I ended up in her husband's Sunday school class. Accident? No, God ordained it all. Each Sunday morning in class, requests were made for volunteers to help at the center. And each time, I felt as though the Lord was saying to me, "I want you to go there." I refused. I just wanted to get on with my new life. This continued until one morning, following still another call for help, I asked for a volunteer application. In my heart, I told the Lord that I would respond, but under the condition that I would not have to tell my secret to anyone. That was my deal. Working at the center might help me feel better about myself, I reasoned. I thought that was what I needed to be able to forgive myself and move past the guilt I still felt.

Following my volunteer training, I was asked to observe a counseling session. The day I arrived for my observation was a particularly busy one. As a result, I was asked to begin a session on my own with a young girl, until an experienced counselor could join us. I felt comfortable with the idea and agreed. It was quickly apparent that this girl was abortion minded, so I began sharing all I learned in training. Nothing seemed to touch her. She had made up her mind. I felt the Lord prompting me to share my testimony with her. I kept reminding the Lord of our deal: no telling of secrets. Finally, I surrendered and began telling her of my experience. As I did, the tears began rolling down her cheeks; she was actually listening now. God confirmed right then, "This is why I brought you here. These girls and women need to know the pain sin brings. They need to know the truth about abortion."

Midway into my testimony, the Associate Director of the clinic, unaware of my abortion history, entered the room. She heard my story, too. After the girl left, she and I had a wonderful time of crying and praising the Lord together. This was the beginning of radical change in my life. That night I felt so free; I was no longer the guardian of my dark secret. It was as if a weight had been lifted from my shoulders; I was no longer living a lie. At the time the best part for me was realizing that this co-laborer didn't think any less of me because of what I had done. She was full of love and compassion, and it overwhelmed me. God took my greatest fears and showed me that He would not leave me alone.

A year later, I completed a post-abortion recovery Bible study, offered at the clinic. The Lord really transformed my life through that study. Up until that time I had been making some progress, opening up a little more at a time; but through the study, He brought down all the walls - the walls of shame and guilt that blocked forgiveness. I can never adequately explain what took place in my heart and life, but I can tell you that I was set free from the chains that bound me to my horrible past! For 10 years I carried so much guilt and shame in my heart, believing God would never use me. Satan convinced me I was useless and unworthy to be called a Christian. The day that I realized the truth of Romans 8:1 that, **"There is therefore now no condemnation for those who are in Christ Jesus."** was the happiest day of my life. I thank God for His forgiveness and the precious promises He gives us. I've never been the same since.

During this period of cleansing in my life, God also did a great work in my marriage. He gave me the courage to tell my husband the truth about my adulterous relationship and the baby I had carried for a short time. God in His mercy, moved to restore the integrity of our relationship and to strengthen the lifetime commitment we had made to one another. In the course of that sweet time of honesty and forgiveness, the Lord taught me how to look to Him - rather than to a human relationship - to satisfy my deepest longings for love and acceptance. At last, the dishonesty that had long driven my life and my decisions was replaced with truth and freedom from the guilt that enslaved me.

Two years later, on her sixteenth birthday I had the opportunity to share what God had done in my life with my daughter, Tevon. During a mother-daughter getaway weekend, the Lord provided time for us to share and challenge each other to a pure and whole-hearted walk with Christ. That precious time together is a testimony to the deep transformation God had accomplished in me over the years. It marked the beginning of a ministry that would allow me to openly tell other women about the pain of abortion, along with the life-giving forgiveness that can only be found in Christ.

Each day God gives me joy in relaying my testimony of God's forgiveness to hurting women. I love to help them realize there is hope after an abortion. As though this were not enough, there is great joy in knowing that God is pleased to use broken vessels that he has mended. He not only forgave me and made me a new person, but, for the past 12 years, He has allowed me to be a part of the process of helping other women by leading the post-abortion ministry in my hometown. I get to watch in amazement as God frees woman after woman from the guilt of her past, just as He did for me.

Only God can take our greatest sins and work them together for good! If abortion is what it took for me to find Jesus, then I'm thankful for it all - the pain, the guilt, the anguish. The joy, peace and forgiveness far outweigh the suffering. As the Bible says in Luke 7:47, **"For this reason I say to you, her sins, which are many, have been forgiven, for she loved much; but he who is forgiven little, loves little."** I have been forgiven for so many sins. I love the Lord with my whole heart and soul because I realize the depths to which He reached down to rescue me. My greatest desire is to give Him all the glory for what He has done for me.

Chris's Update:
Today literally thousands have heard Chris' story. Chris is leader of the post-abortion recovery Bible study offered at Charlotte Pregnancy Care Center, in Charlotte, NC. She and her husband Mark reside in Charlotte, which is also home to their now married daughter and her family. If you would like to meet Chris, she generally attends our Women's Discipleship Retreats every fall and makes herself available to post-abortive women.

Personally to you...
1. How were you encouraged after reading Chris's story?

2. At what point(s) did you identify with her story?

3. Below are a few Scripture passages Chris used. Which one(s) could you apply to your circumstance(s)? How do they help you?

    • Romans 8:1

    • Luke 7:47

Day 23

Our God is an awesome God and He is at work even now to bring comfort to your spirit and strength to your life. As God has brought many post-abortive women across my path, I have found several verses that have been helpful to these women. I have written these verses in the back of my Bible. As I share them with you, I trust they will bring you hope in your pain. Maybe you would like to write these same verses in your Bible, so that one day you will be ready to share God's comfort with a woman in need who He brings across your path. (2 Corinthians 1:3-5) Then you can pass on the hope you have received in Jesus Christ through His Word. Following are some Scripture verses you can apply to abortion. Write a few key words from each passage:

- Romans 8:1

- Isaiah 12:2

- Ezekial 36:26

- Psalm 32:1-5

- Psalm 51:10-17

- Psalm 103:8-12

- Psalm 107:14-15

- John 8:32,36

- 1 John 3:19-20

- Isaiah 43:18-19

- Romans 6:21-22

- Hebrews 10:17-18

I hope these verses mean as much to you as they have meant to me over the years. I pray that God will use you to share His comfort with other women. I send my love to each of you as you persevere in this study! I promise it will be worth every tear shed, every page turned, and all the time you have spent! Press on, my dear friend.

Chapter 6

"For I know the plans that I have for you,
declares the Lord, plans for welfare and not
for calamity to give you a future and a hope."
Jeremiah 29:11

Hope for the Future

God's Principles for Living in the Future

Day 24

Hope for the Future

As you read the stories of lives that were radically affected by their decision to have an abortion, at least three elements were evident in restoring their lives. First, their recognition that God forgives sin, including the sin of abortion, confessing that sin and accepting God's forgiveness freed them from the guilt of their past. Second, as they began to live in God's forgiveness, they were able to forgive others who had hurt them and reconciled relationships within their families. Third, their lives took on meaning and hope as they discovered the purpose God had for them and were able to use their experience of God's forgiving grace to help others. Each of these stories included these elements but as you can see it took time and the process was different in each of their lives.

Forgiveness, reconciliation, and purpose for living all flow out of a loving relationship with God. We can obtain forgiveness because God loves us and sent His Son to die in our place. We are reconciled to God when we turn from our own selfish ways and receive God's loving gift of forgiveness through His Son. Our response to that love is to reflect God's love by forgiving others. The only reasonable response to being loved is to love in return and that love gives meaning to life. When we love God, we show it by giving of ourselves both to God and to others. In Matthew 22:37-39 Jesus summed up the motive for all our relationships and activities in two commands, " **'You shall love the Lord your God with all your heart, and with all your soul, and with all your mind.'** "**This is the great and foremost commandment.** "**The second is like it, 'You shall love your neighbor as yourself.'** "

Read Luke 7:36-39, 44-46
To see the basis of our love for God, lets turn to Luke 7:36-50 and see the contrast in one who has received Jesus' forgiveness and one who only wants to put Him to the test.

1. How are the two people in the room with Jesus different from one another? (vs. 36-37).

2. What was the Pharisee's opinion of Jesus and the woman? (vs. 39).

3. What did this woman's actions toward Jesus indicate? How do you think she had the nerve to come into the presence of the sinless Son of God? What kind of encounter must she have previously had with Jesus to give her confidence to enter Simon's house?

4. Have you ever felt unworthy of coming to God or that your sin was too great for Him to forgive? Is there anything or anywhere that you can hide from God? See Psalm 139:1-4, 7-12.

Because Psalm 139:3 says that God is intimately acquainted with ALL our ways, He already knows every detail of your life. Since He died for the sins of the world, the only sin that cannot be forgiven is the sin of unbelief (John 3:18). So, would there be anything that you have done that God could not forgive? Write out the following verses:

• Matthew 19:26b

• Jeremiah 32:17, 27

What is the basis of God's forgiveness - His character or our worthiness? Is there anything we can do to deserve God's forgiveness or make up for our sinful deeds?

• Proverbs 14:12

• Isaiah 64:6

• Acts 10:43

• Ephesians 2:8-9

• Titus 3:5

So, what if you do not feel forgiven? Who are you questioning? Is God faithful to his promise? Have you asked for forgiveness? Are you sincere about turning from your sin? If you have truly repented, asked for forgiveness, and forgiven those who have hurt you, then write out Romans 8:1 because it applies to you.

If you have fulfilled God's requirements for forgiveness and still feel unforgiven then your feelings may pridefully be demanding a higher standard than God for forgiveness. Feelings are the result of the way you think. When your feelings do not agree with what you know to be true, you must renew your mind with God's Word. In that way you must continually inform your feelings with the truth of God's Word using verses such as Romans 8:1.

As this immoral woman in our story faced her sin and found forgiveness, her focus was on demonstrating her love for Jesus.

1. Jesus points out how a host would ordinarily treat his guest by contrasting the behavior of his host and the uninvited guest. What three things were considered common courtesy? (vs. 44-46).

2. How did this forgiven woman go beyond the common custom of the day? What did her extravagant display indicate? (vs. 44-47).

3. What was the basis of her love?

4. What does Jesus say was the reason for the difference in their behavior towards Him? (vs. 47).

The Pharisee did not see his need for forgiveness but considered himself righteous. The prostitute who was forgiven all her sins demonstrated her overwhelming love for Jesus by washing His feet with her tears and wiping His feet with her hair. Jesus understood that her actions flowed out of her heart of love and gratitude to Him because she had been forgiven so much. We often think of love as a feeling, but love is expressed by our actions. God is the originator of love. In fact I John 4:8 says, **"God is love."** So we must learn from God what love is. God demonstrated what love does when He died for us while we were sinners (Romans 5:8). God so loved the world that He gave His only Son. God shows that love is the sacrificial giving of oneself for the benefit of the one loved. Jesus said, **"If you love Me, you will keep My commandments."** As in any love relationship, our love relationship with God will require our time and our loyalty to demonstrate our sincerity.

Just the word "love" carries a ring of hope. Where there is love there is joy and peace and understanding and comfort. The real source of our hope is our loving God and His trustworthy promises. First of all He says that He has given us everything we need to live life on this earth and to grow spiritually. 2 Peter 1:3-4 says:

> **"His divine power has granted to us everything pertaining to life and godliness, through the true knowledge of Him who called us by His own glory and excellence. For by these He has granted to us His precious and magnificent promises, in order that by them you might become partakers of the divine nature, having escaped the corruption that is in the world by lust."**

So with God and His Word as our resource, our hope is not just a "hope so" attitude, but it is as sure as the character of God who gives us His Word. Hebrews 11:1 says, **"Now faith is the assurance of things hoped for, the conviction of things not seen."** Our hope is born out of assurance that God is faithful to fulfill all that He has promised and the conviction that His Word is always true.

Because understanding and accepting God's forgiveness is such a milestone for a woman who has had an abortion, some women find it helpful to have a tangible reminder of their new-found freedom.

You may wish to write a letter here to God to express your love and thanksgiving for the mercy He has shown to you.

Day 25

Please read 2 Peter 1:2-9.

1. Grace and peace are multiplied to you in knowing God. What is it that God has granted to meet all your needs in verses 3 and 4?

2. Where can you find "the true knowledge of Him" and "His precious and magnificent promises?"

3. What will it require of you to obtain what God has granted? (Verse 5).

4. List and define the seven qualities that we are to supply with diligent effort.

   A.

   B.

   C.

   D.

   E.

   F.

   G.

5. What will these qualities help you to become? (Verse 8).

6. What does verse 8 say the lack of these qualities will reveal about your memory?

How wonderful it is that our usefulness and fruitfulness for God are not limited by the sins we have committed in the past. It is only as we forget the magnitude of the forgiveness we have received that we slack in our diligence and become useless and unfruitful. Remembering what Christ has done for you keeps your love for Him strong. Maintaining that love relationship requires time, loyalty, and perseverance. Just as people need to spend time together communicating honestly with one another in order to know each other well, our relationship with God can only grow as we spend time in His Word getting to know Him and communicating with Him in prayer. If knowing God is a relationship and not an event, then it will require constant attention and diligence as we learned in 2 Peter 1:5. What steps will you take to make God's Word and prayer a part of your daily life?

Day 26

Once we recognize, repent and confess our sin, it is our responsibility to set a plan in motion so that we do not return to that sin. As a Christian our response to being forgiven is to love God and desire to please Him in all that we do. I know I cannot allow myself to be exposed to sexual things on television or in movies because of my past. You may need to change some things to avoid temptation as well. The changes required to show our love for God by living in a way that is pleasing to Him will require our diligent effort. Since for much of our lives we have been going our own way and living to please ourselves, our sinful habits have become so ingrained that we respond to life's situations without even thinking. To make the radical change our minds must be renewed with God's Word. Then we can put off our sinful ways of thinking and have God's perspective in order to change our behavior.

Read Ephesians 4:20-32
1. Now that you have learned the truth in Jesus, what do you see that it was that corrupted your former manner of living, according to Ephesians 4:22? (Remember Eve's desires?)

2. What three things does Paul tell you to do in verses 22-24 (look for the verbs)?

3. What qualities in verse 24 characterize the "new self"?

4. List the things from verses 25-32 that must change when you put-off the "old self" and put-on the "new self." You may add to the list as God reveals things to you from other Scriptures.

Put Off

1. vs. 25-Lying

2.

3.

4.

5.

6.

7.

Put On

1. Speaking truth only

2.

3.

4.

5.

6.

7.

5. What specific sins in your life do you know you need to put-off now?

We have talked about the pride involved in hiding your abortion, the lack of forgiveness in blaming others, the bitterness and anger associated with your abortion, and the sinful thoughts that have rationalized and justified your behavior. As you view these things in light of God's Word and seek His forgiveness, He will enable you to put on His righteous standard for living. God will not ask you to do anything without giving you the strength to carry it out. Just remember, as you seek to live pleasing to God, He will enable you to obey what He has asked you to do.

Stop! Take time to go through your list of "put offs" listed in question 5. Confess your sins to God, asking for His help in putting on godly character. (Philippians 4:13)

6. Now that you have renewed your mind with God's Word, what must you "put on" to replace each of your sinful practices? Find a scripture for each new habit to "put on."

Put Off	Put On
1. Bitterness and Resentment	1. Kindness and Forgiveness (Ephesians 4:32).
2.	2.
3.	3.
4.	4.
5.	5.

7. What will you do to keep yourself from returning to your old habits and to develop the new godly habits? Suggestions:

- Write out the verse describing the godly behavior and place it where you will see it often.
- Make yourself accountable to a godly person.
- Determine the things do you need to eliminate (T.V. programs, magazines, radio, music, etc...) from your life or home to discourage ungodly ways?
- Determine what you need to add (regular attendance at a Bible teaching church, daily time in God's Word and prayer, memorizing appropriate Scripture, godly friends, discernment in music, reading, and listening, etc.) to your life or home to increase your godly ways?
- Circle those things you will begin to do to develop your new walk with God.

Day 27

Studying God's Word is the key to renewing the mind and developing a God-honoring life. We must learn God's ways and do them in order to please our loving heavenly Father. As you progress in your Christian walk, it is helpful to keep a "journal" of truths God is teaching you, of ways God has protected you, of ways you recognize His grace to you, and of ways He provides for your needs. As you keep a record of all your personal blessings you will be able to see the progress of your walk with God and remember from where you have come.

Several years ago, I prepared a prayer journal called *In Everything By Prayer* that can help you develop and record your walk through life with God. This notebook provides pages for writing prayers of praise, thanksgiving, confession, supplication, intercession and more. As you record God's answers to your prayer, your faith will be strengthened by God's faithfulness. Included in the journal is a best-loved section on "How to pray for your Husband/Children." See the back of this book for ordering information.

Another way that God has renewed my mind is by memorizing Scripture. I do not know where I would be today without disciplining myself to memorize God's Word. The time spent memorizing and meditating on God's Word has been used by God to change my heart (Psalm 119:11, 105; Romans 12:1, 2). All through my Christian life, especially after my first husband died, I placed God's Word in my memory bank so that I could find His comfort and strength through His Word at a moments notice. After experiencing His sustaining power at that time in my life, I have never forgotten the importance of the Word in my daily life. God has enabled me by His grace to memorize seven whole books of the Bible that I continually review (2 Timothy; Colossians; James; 2 Peter; Philemon; Jude; and Philippians). God's Word is still transforming my mind as it instructs, reproves, corrects, and trains me in righteousness (2 Timothy 3:16).

I have included the guidelines that I use to memorize in the back of this book. Turn to it and read through the guidelines (Appendix I). I have used an acrostic of the word promise. I hope you will accept the challenge to memorize God's Word and be blessed as I have been (Psalm 119:11,105). You could begin by choosing Scriptures from the studies in this book that have special meaning to you. Remember, it is the truth that sets you free (John 8:32). Tomorrow we will look at ways that God can transform your heart.

Day 28

Turn to Colossians 3:12-17 to see some of the ways God wants to transform your heart. When the Scripture speaks of the heart, it is not merely speaking of the emotions, but of the thoughts and the will of man. To whom is this passage speaking?

1. Who can be described as "chosen," "holy," and "beloved" by God?

2. What are the five attitudes in verse 12 that should characterize the believer's heart in relation to others? Define each one.

    A.

    B.

    C.

    D.

    E.

3. What are two actions that would demonstrate the right heart attitudes? (vs.13)

4. What has God done for you to prepare your heart to forgive others? (vs. 13).

5. Colossians 3:14 speaks of love's bond of unity. List the ways love promotes unity from I Corinthians 13:4-8.

The next three verses describe how love should manifest itself among believers.

Colossians 3:15-17 says, **"And let the peace of Christ rule in your hearts, to which indeed you were called in one body and be thankful. Let the Word of Christ richly dwell within you, with all wisdom teaching and admonishing one another with psalms and hymns and spiritual songs, singing with thankfulness in your hearts to God. And whatever you do in word or deed, do all in the name of the Lord Jesus, giving thanks through Him to God the Father."**

List the two commands that begin with "let."

1.

2.

Peace comes from living out your love for God and others by putting on the godly qualities of Colossians 3:12-13 and remembering what God has done in forgiving you.

6. What heart attitude in Colossians 3:15-16 needs to be present to obey these commands?

7. In what ways are you thankful for the things you have learned from getting God's perspective on your abortion?

It is not by accident that you received this book, whether you ordered it or a dear friend gave it to you. It is because of God's great love for you that He did not want you to live with your silent pain or to remain in your shame and guilt. Your heart's attitude should turn to thankfulness as God's perspective on your abortion has unfolded. You have seen God's promise to remember your sin no more. When he forgives your sin, it is removed as far as the east is from the west, and His lovingkindness for His children is everlasting. When you have received God's forgiveness you can only respond in thankfulness for your release from sin and despair. As you discipline yourself for the purpose of Godliness (1 Timothy 4:7), God will transform your life to walk in light of the peace and love He gives.

8. When Colossians 3:16 says "let the Word of Christ dwell in you richly," how will that be reflected in the way you talk with the ones closest to you? How is the Word of God likely to come out in your speech?

9. How do the following scriptures reveal the purpose for all that we do as believers?

- Colossians 3:17

- 1 Corinthians 10:31

- 2 Corinthians 5:15

Just as God's faithfulness encourages our faith, our loyalty to Him is expressed in thankfulness, obedience, and service. James 1:22 warns us that we delude ourselves if we think we know God just because we have heard His Word. Unless we do what God's Word tells us to do, our religion is worthless and we are disloyal to Christ. I encourage you to find a Bible teaching church where you can grow in your knowledge of the Lord and also where you can be accountable to others. To obey God you must be in fellowship with other believers as you seek to live for Him. Hebrews 10:25 (NIV) says, **"Let us not give up meeting together, as some are in the habit of doing, but let us encourage one another - and all the more as you see the Day approaching."** Make it a priority to be worshiping God in a Bible-teaching church that will help you grow in your relationship with Him.

Chapter 7

"Thou wilt make known to me the path of life;
In Thy presence is fullness of joy;
In thy right hand there are pleasures forever."
Psalm 16:11

A Closing Word

Day 29

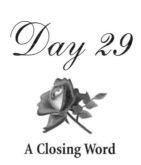

A Closing Word

Well, dear friends, we have been through a lot together. I am sure, like me, you have shed many tears. I hurt for you even now as I think of you reading, writing, and coming to terms with your own personal guilt, shame, and heartache. I hope you will prayerfully read on to the end of this chapter. In many ways, I feel as if I have relived many of the challenges I went through when I truly understood the forgiveness of God. That time in my life brought so many changes. It is exciting now to look back and see how very much God loved me to help me see His plan for my life. I want to end this chapter with three verses that have been of immeasurable help to me. I pray they will be an encouragement to you as you seek to live in His forgiveness from this day forward.

Three Bible verses have guided me through my Christian life for as long as I can remember. I was 23 years old when my first husband died and I distinctly remember my precious grandmother giving me Romans 8:28. It says, **"we know that in all things God works for the good of those who love him, who have been called according to His purpose" (NIV).** There was a time when I did not even want to believe that God could bring good out of my abortion. I now know that the good He intended was to bring me to repentance and conformity to His Son, Jesus Christ. The second verse, Jeremiah 29:11, assures me that God actually has plans for my life. Yes, even after I sinned He had plans to use my life to share His love with others. My third verse, my life verse, is Psalm 16:11. It gives me God's assurance that in His presence He will show me the path of life where there is fullness of joy. God used these three verses to give me hope and to bring me through the joyful pain of getting right with Him.

Lets take the next few minutes and unravel the precious truths in Romans 8:28. Go back and re-read the verse again. Who works all things together for good? Of course, God does! Do you think this includes your abortion? Well, let's look again. How many things does God work together for good? What about our sin, suffering, pain, and temptation, are those things supposed to work together for our good? You are exactly right - everything is included. God says, "all things." For whom does God do this? Take a look at the whole verse because the answer is there. It says, **"God works all things together for good to those who love Him, who have been called according to His purpose."** Yes, it is only for those who *love* God. It is for those of us who have placed our faith and hope in the Lord Jesus and called on His name in repentance. Someone who is "called according to His purpose" is someone who is born again into that blessed new hope found only in a relationship with Jesus Christ. God's purpose for making us His own is that we might become more like His Son. He continually works in our lives to help us strive toward the goal of Christlikeness.

Well, my friend, that verse my grandmother gave me many years ago has had a major impact on my life today. When I look at that verse, I know that God has worked the sin of my abortion together for my good and for His glory. Do I feel badly about what I did? I have grieved over my sin, but I no longer live with the guilt and shame of my sin because Jesus Christ has forgiven me (Matthew 5:4).

This second verse has equally impacted my life because it tells me that God has always had a plan for my life. For years I believed that because I had had an abortion, God would never want to use my life for His glory. The verse is Jeremiah 29:11:

> **"For I know the plans I have for you, declares the Lord,**
> **plans for welfare and not for calamity to give you a**
> **future and a hope."**

Just as God had plans to give Israel a future hope of blessing in the land, He has shown me that He has plans of future blessing for me by using my life for His glory. His great mercy was extended to me to demonstrate His forgiving love. God knew that I would go through much suffering because of sin, but He did not intend to destroy me, nor was He punishing me. His love and mercy were new every morning for me (Lamentations 3:21-25). You see, God has the big picture and He had a future plan for my life and I found this to be reason for hope. After living with my guilt and shame for so many years, I could hardly believe that I had hope. God sought to bring me to a new place, a place of restoration and hope where I could live in the joy of His forgiveness.

This leads me to this last verse, which is my life verse:

"Thou wilt show me the path of life: in thy presence is fullness of joy; at thy right hand there are pleasures for evermore."
Psalm 16:11 (KJV)

Through His Word, God has shown me the path that He wanted me to take is the path of eternal life. From my study of God's Word, I knew God wanted me to comfort women with the comfort I had found in His Word. He wanted me to share with them about the forgiveness available in Him even after having had an abortion. My true joy is being in His presence now and in eternity. I can honestly say that I have received great pleasure from obediently living in His presence. The joy of being forgiven and of seeing women come to terms with the pain, guilt, shame, and heartache is a joy that is full. *He truly* is working all things together for my good, and in Him I have fullness of joy.

All this is possible because He loves us so much and has the power to fulfill His promises. Romans 8:37-39 says it so well. **"But in all these things we overwhelmingly conquer through Him who loved us. For I am convinced that neither death, nor life, nor angels, nor principalities, nor things present, nor things to come, nor powers, nor height, nor depth, nor any other created thing, shall be able to separate us from the love of God, which is in Christ Jesus our Lord."**

If you have not already done so, won't you take the time right now and pour out your heart to God? Bring Him the sorrow of your sinful past and the resolve in your heart to obey Him. As you confess your sin and turn to Him in repentance, He will cleanse you and release you from the guilt of your sin.

I want to challenge you to write out your commitment to God. Tell Him how much you love Him for what He's done for you. Thank Him for the forgiveness and the hope you now have in Christ. Express your commitment to turn from your own way and live in obedience to Him. As you study God's Word and pray for God to guide you, He will lead you in the path of obedience. My prayers are with you as you live in His forgiveness.

Your commitment to God:

- Express your love to Him by thanking Him for His forgiveness:

- Express your commitment to live in light of His forgiveness:

Day 30

If you wish, use this day to journal your own experience. Describe how the love and mercy of God has enabled you to find forgiveness and to look forward to a future of praise and service to Him.

Appendix

Appendix I
Scripture Memory

Isaiah 55:11 is a **PROMISE** that God's Word will not return void. We have used an acrostic of the word "promise" as a helpful guideline for Scripture memory.

Pray

Pray about what the Lord would have you memorize. Begin with verses that have special meaning for you from this book. Set realistic goals for yourself about how many verses to memorize each week and work on it daily. Eventually you may want to memorize a whole chapter or even a whole book of the Bible.

Repetition

Repetition is the key to effective Scripture memory. Read each verse until you can repeat it without looking. Try repeating verses out loud - it will use another one of your senses. When you have memorized a verse add a new verse to what you have memorized. If you miss a day or two, start where you left off.

Organize

Use 3x5 index cards. Example: Psalm 139 has 24 verses: use 3 index cards and put 8 verses on the card - 4 verses on the front and 4 on the back. Make sure you proof read each verse that you have written on your index cards.

Meditate

Meditate on the words in each verse to understand its meaning and apply it to your life. Repeat the verse slowly emphasizing a different word each time. Look up words to clarify their meaning. Ask yourself what this says about God and how you can use it in your life? Be sure you understand the context's effect on the interpretation.

Inspire

Inspire others by sharing what you are doing. It would help you to be accountable to a person in your church or a family member. Repeat verses to them when you meet. Be encouraging!

Saturate

Saturate your mind with God's Word so it may renew your thinking and you may grow in godly wisdom.

Edify

Edification is to be the purpose of our speech (Ephesians 4:29). As God's Word becomes a part of your life, your edifying words will flow from your renewed mind and bring glory to God in your witness for Him. Trust me, Scripture memory will effectively transform your life.

You may want to start on a few verses that we have listed throughout this book to help you grow stronger in your relationship with the Lord Jesus.

Appendix II

A few words from my husband...

Dear Reader,

As a husband, nothing brings me more joy and satisfaction than serving together with my wife, Sandy, as we walk in the path that God has called us to in service through Caleb Ministries. Sandy's labors of writing, speaking, and serving are exemplary! Ephesians 2:10 sums up the goal of every Christian for their salvation - to walk in the "good works" that God has decreed. It states, **"For we are His workmanship, created in Christ Jesus for good works, which God prepared beforehand so that we should walk in them."**

Post-abortive women need other women guiding them through the Scriptures to work through their silent pain. God's Word, the Bible, is sufficient to administer the comfort that is needed by those whose lives have been affected by an abortion. Sandy has written this book to facilitate that learning and growth progression. *Living in His Forgiveness* is the fruit of her life's work to the glory of God.

She will always be my P-31 (Proverbs 31) wife.

Walking in His plans,

Craig Day
Co-Founder of Caleb Ministries along with my dear wife.

Appendix III

CALEB HISTORY

Over the years, our volunteers have been blessed to watch as God comforts and restores broken and hurting women through Caleb Ministries as well as its Outreach Ministries. It has been a journey.

On Sunday August 5, 1990, sitting in the choir loft of her church, Sandy realized that God wanted her to comfort others in their loss with the comfort she had received from God. Her heart ached to share God's comfort with women like herself who had suffered deep, painful losses. In 1988 Craig and Sandy had experienced God's comfort during the loss of their precious son, Caleb. In the days that followed, both she and her husband gave prayerful consideration to the organization of a ministry to others who were experiencing sorrow. That ministry would be named in memory of their much loved and missed son.

In the early days of Caleb Ministries, Sandy had many opportunities to travel and share her testimony of God's comfort through His Word. Sandy's transparent truthfulness about her struggles impacted the lives of countless women who have attended these conferences and retreats.

After only one year of ministry, Caleb Ministries expanded to include a personal one-on-one ministry to women who had experienced miscarriage, stillbirth, early infant death or infertility. The story of Caleb in Numbers 13 and 14 from which the name Caleb Cares emerged, provided insight for this ministry to the sorrowing. It was at this time that Caleb Ministries became a 501(c)(3) non-profit Christian organization.

Even as Sandy was ministering to other women, God continued His convicting work in her life. Through His Word, God showed her that in order to minister to others, she would have to allow every area of her life to be exposed to the light of His truth. God continually exposed hidden areas that required her repentant confession in her growing walk with God. As she responded to God's refining fire, the ministry grew with her.

One of the outgrowths of this responsiveness to God was a prayer journal called In Everything By Prayer (see website) that Sandy developed with her friend Donna Peters. Through the years, God has used this unique tool to encourage women to have a more consistent prayer life. With over

15,000 copies of the journal in print, many families have been blessed. The most popular section of the journal entitled "How to pray for your Husband/Children," has helped many women support their families with effective prayer.

In 1993, two years into the ministry of Caleb Cares, Sandy compiled nine stories of individuals who had experienced the loss of a child and received God's restoring grace into the book entitled Morning Will Come. Volunteers scanned the obituaries of local papers and sent copies of the book to women who had lost children. The response was overwhelming. With 10,000 copies in print, letters came from women around the world with testimony to the encouragement it had brought to them.

Caleb Cares chapters began forming across the U.S. by 1995. Each chapter began by providing copies of Morning Will Come to hurting women in their areas. It was also during this time that a Caleb Ministries Women's Discipleship Retreat was organized. Each year since then women attend from all over the country to hear outstanding Bible teaching and find encouragement. It never fails to be a time of spiritual renewal for all who attend.

In was the summer of 1995, God brought still another dimension to Caleb Ministries. God led nine women to call the ministry who had lost babies, each indicating that they had experienced a prior abortion. As Sandy ministered to these women she realized God wanted to use her own abortion, at age 19, to help other women. In response to God's conviction, Sandy confessed her abortion to her father, opening the door for complete family restoration. Through this difficult time, God prepared Sandy to talk publicly about the short and long-term affects of abortion. Her story exposes long held secrets and touches those who hear of the forgiving power of God.

A second manuscript used by Caleb Ministries was completed in 1998. The devotional journal, The Memories I Cherish, was developed by Sandy Day together with Donna Elyea. This beautifully presented keepsake provides a place to record the journey of one's walk with God through their time of loss. It serves to help them remember the comfort and encouragement they received in the years to come.

The P.A.T. (Providing A Treasure) Ministry began with a passion to assist a grieving woman or couple in a loving, yet practical way. The P.A.T. box includes a burial gown, bonnet, blanket, as well as a Caleb Cares brochure, an envelope to hold a lock of the baby's hair, and a copy of Morning Will Come. These items are wrapped in acid-free tissue paper and tucked in a precious box that parents will treasure through the years. P.A.T. boxes are provided to hospitals and funeral homes across the United States, and make their way into the arms of those who, tragically, have no child to bring home. The boxes are also available by individual request.

Abbey's Place, our post-abortion ministry, got underway in 1999. Its goal is to provide support and guidance to women who are struggling with the guilt, pain, and grief of a past abortion decision. Our hope is that each person God sends to us will achieve spiritual and emotional restoration through Christ.

In January of 2000, Craig Day followed his call to seminary, moving with his family to California. The ministry continually grew by leaps and bounds as a West Coast Chapter began and a Caleb Ministries web site was constructed in order to make materials and contact information available to women everywhere. It is a blessing to see God use technology to distribute much needed assistance on-line! Craig graduated in May 2002 from the Master's Seminary in Sun Valley, CA and is now pastoring a church.

Caleb Chapters continue to form in other states, as God raises up godly leaders in local churches with a vision to minister to those weighted down by grief or guilt. We stand amazed at the way God burdens women to minister to women, and at the way He intervenes to make all things possible.

Since its beginnings in 1990, Caleb Ministries has flourished as God has led us as individuals, as Chapters, and as an international ministry. Faithful men and women, hand-picked by the Father, serve as Board of Directors, ministry coordinators, and volunteers. We count it a privilege to continually help women who are struggling with difficult seasons and situations and to nurture them in the ways of the Lord - the only One who can truly help and heal.

Our commitment: *"...ministering to hearts...seeing God change lives"*

Appendix IV

How We Minister

The Mission of Caleb Ministries is to reach people with the gospel of Jesus Christ and to establish them in right relationship with Him, according to the Word of God, through compassionate outreach, teaching, biblical counsel, and discipleship.

Ministry Outreaches

Sandy Day's Speaking Ministry
Sandy Day is an exciting speaker with a ministering heart. God uses her to draw people to Christ because of her love for God's Word and for others to be helped by it. Sandy's enthusiasm for Christ is contagious - her love for Jesus abounds. Sandy and her husband Craig are Founders of Caleb Ministries. She is available for speaking engagements/women's conferences. Her testimony is available online.

Caleb Cares
This outreach ministry provides support and encouragement to women who are struggling with the trauma of infertility, miscarriage, stillbirth, and early infant death. Volunteers who have suffered similar experiences are paired one-on-one with clients. They offer the compassion of a friend who understands grief and the comfort that Jesus Christ provides through His Word. Also, Caleb Chapters have been formed across the U.S. If you would like to inquire about a chapter or are interested in starting one in your city, please e-mail the ministry at info@calebministries.org and guidelines will be sent to you. Just recently we put together a "Miscarriage Bag" called "Especially for You." Included in this beautiful organdy bag is a helpful booklet, a stained glass angel, and a beautiful handkerchief for her tears. If you have a friend who has experienced a miscarriage, these items can be puchased on our web site.

The P.A.T. Ministry (Providing A Treasure)
This outreach ministry provides beautiful memorial boxes to women who have experienced a stillbirth or early infant death. The boxes contain a burial gown, a blanket, a bonnet, and a copy of Morning Will Come. They may be kept and used as a treasure box for the baby's memorabilia. They are distributed to churches, hospitals, and doctors' offices, as well as by direct request.

<u>Abbey's Place</u>
This outreach ministry provides support and guidance to women who are struggling with the guilt, pain, and grief of an abortion decision. *Living in His Forgiveness* is offered through small group Bible studies or individually with clients.

<u>Women's Discipleship Retreats</u>
Every fall women gather from across the U.S. to hear God's relevant Word and share warm fellowship at our life-changing Women's Discipleship Retreats at Springmaid Beach, SC (South Myrtle Beach). The purposes of our retreats are to firmly root, build up, and establish Christian women in the truth of God's Word (Colossians 2:6-7). Call our ministry for this year's brochure. You will be blessed!

To contact us:

Sandy Day
C/O Caleb Ministries
PO Box 470093
Charlotte, NC 28247
1-877-4U-CALEB OR (704) 544-1320

Sandy is available for Women's Conferences and Retreats. Visit our website at <u>www.calebministries.org.</u> Email us at: <u>info@calebministries.org</u> for additional help or information.

Also, every fall Caleb Ministries has a Women's Discipleship Retreat at Springmaid Beach, SC (South Myrtle Beach, SC). E-mail us at retreat@caleb-ministries.org for this year's brochure.

Appendix V

Suggested format for Small Group Bible Study

If you are planning to use *Living in His Forgiveness* for a small group Bible Study, we would like to suggest a few things that will be of help to you:

1. It needs to be a small group. Maybe 4-5 women including the facilitator/group leader. Each class will last 2 hours.
2. The Bible study should be held in a place where there would be no interruptions. You will need to ask the women the first night to turn off cell phones/pagers/etc... If the Bible study is in a home ask the host to turn the ringers off of their phones.
3. Each woman needs to be committed for the entire study. If she misses a week it would be helpful for her to meet with the group leader to make it up before the next meeting.
4. You will need to determine the number of lessons you wish to complete each week. Since the length varies, you may determine this on a week-by-week basis. It would be helpful to go through each portion of the study.
5. Always be certain to begin and end each session in prayer. Commit to supporting one another in prayer throughout the week ahead.
   - Week 1: Give out book or have them purchase the book through their local Christian bookstore. Invite each woman to share her story with the group, as she is comfortable in doing so. Stress that information shared at the Bible study must be kept confidential so that a circle of trust may be established. If there is time, suggest that class members share their expectations for the course. Close in prayer.
   - Week 2: Discuss the testimonies in Chapter 1 and share reactions and lessons learned through the Scriptures given. Determine by class end the number of lesson days to be completed before the next session.
   - Week 3: Discuss an overview of the assigned lessons. Share specifically answers that are objective in nature; answers that may vary and would generate group participation. Encourage women to share with one another, but never put anyone on the spot to contribute.
   - Weeks 4: (or as many as you desire). Continue at a pace that is comfortable with the group.

I would suggest an 8-week study. The book is distributed the first week. Some chapters are longer than others. The last week could conclude with each participant sharing Day 3o.